67-23122 (11·13·67)

THE MANCHESTER AFFAIR

THE
MANCHESTER
AFFAIR

by John Corry

G. P. Putnam's Sons
New York

Copyright © 1967 by John Corry

*Library of Congress Catalog
Card Number: 67-23122*

FOR
Agnes and John Corry

Introduction

~~~~

O N December 16, 1966, Mrs. John F. Kennedy filed a suit
    to prevent the publication of *The Death of a President,*
a book she once authorized in the interest of accuracy and
dignity, but which she then found to be tasteless and distorted. She named Harper & Row, Cowles Communications,
and William Manchester as defendants, and as all the world
now knows she forced them to make changes in both the
book and its serialization. Actually, the passages that offended
her were not very important; they were not even very interesting. What was interesting and what was important were that
the passages were discarded amid an extraordinary amount of
passion and publicity, and that, when the book itself was
published, otherwise sensible and even eminent men criticized it as if it were not a book at all; by then it had a life of
its own, just as did the controversy that surrounded it, and
the sensible and eminent men were choosing sides.

Partly, of course, this was because Robert F. Kennedy and
Lyndon B. Johnson were involved, and politics hung over
the dispute like a cloud, and partly it was because the book
told of the death of John Kennedy. But mostly, I think, it was

because of the extraordinary relationship between America and the Kennedys. I do not know of what stuff this relationship is made, or why it is as it is, but certainly it is there. Jackie is a national preoccupation, and Bobby is nearly so, and sometimes it is a little silly, and sometimes it is a little morbid.

The controversy over *The Death of a President* was a little silly, and sometimes it was a little morbid, too. It joined together celebrated people who rather liked one another and then locked them in something like a tragic embrace, surrounding them at the same time with concentric circles of spokesmen, advisers, sycophants, and reporters. As a reporter writing about the argument, I knew that even the outermost circle could be exhilarating, and I suspect that for some of the people in the innermost circle the exhilaration was great indeed. Perhaps this is what made *The Death of a President* the impossible argument it was and led to the odd financial arrangements between the Kennedys, Harper & Row, and Manchester; it was not every day that all those people could be that close to the Kennedys, even if it was only to dislike them.

"It was as if she were Marie Antoinette, completely isolated from the world around her by her court, her advisers," Manchester said of Jackie Kennedy after he had been discharged from the court. "I only do business with people who are warm and sympathetic," Mrs. Kennedy said, explaining why she would not talk to an executive from *Look* magazine. Indeed, she does not have to do otherwise, and neither does Robert Kennedy. They may pick and choose, and apparently they do, and they are a little spoiled. They are also two of America's great commodities, public property really, which means that nearly everyone thinks they own a piece of them, and nearly everyone wants to know all about them, and Mrs. Kennedy, at least, never seems quite sure if she thinks this is a good thing or a bad thing. It was really a mistake for either one of them, but particularly Mrs. Kennedy, to have got mixed up with Bill Manchester; his was a style entirely different from theirs, far too exotic for them, and when they could not direct him they began to fight him. It was sad all around.

THE MANCHESTER AFFAIR

One

_____~~~_____

W HEN the *Queen Mary* slips into New York Harbor on winter mornings before dawn it is a little like a cheery, fading hotel that is preparing itself for something important; a gathering of governors perhaps, or a visit by someone's prime minister. The hotel, of course, has been through it all before and the staff knows exactly what must be done; mostly it is the guests who are excited. The stewards pile the luggage in mounds, the harbor pilot climbs to the bridge, the deckhands put on clean uniforms. The immigrations and health officers, who reach the ship on a Coast Guard cutter, eat breakfast on their feet in a cramped galley while an apprentice cook in a T-shirt frets over a stove. Passengers stand at the rail and stare at dark Manhattan. The very young and the very old look excited; the teen-agers and young adults do not. Somewhere on board there is at least one celebrity (before jet flights there would have been more) who wonders if there are reporters at dockside. Somewhere, too, there is at least one young woman who is in the way of becoming a celebrity, or who wants to be in the way of becoming one. She also wonders about reporters; perhaps she will find one.

Before the sun rose on December 13, 1966, while tugboats nudged the *Queen Mary* into her pier on the West Side of Manhattan, a man sat alone in a lounge for cabin-class passengers. He was William Manchester, and he had written a book called *The Death of a President*. A little earlier, a Cunard Line official, deferring to the protocol with which his company protects celebrated passengers, had tapped on his door and told him I had reached the ship aboard the Coast Guard cutter and that I wanted to speak to him. Manchester politely declined. He was, he said, under a legal obligation to a London publisher not to speak to reporters. He told the man from Cunard that he hoped I would understand, but there was simply nothing he could do about it. Later, he said, he would get in touch with me if he wanted to make a statement.

Four days earlier, a story in the Chicago *Daily News* had said that Mrs. John F. Kennedy was dismayed by the book Manchester had written. The story recalled that nearly three years before she had asked Manchester to write the one, true, and accurate account of President Kennedy's assassination, and now, it said, she regretted it. She believed that Manchester had abused her confidence, flouted her trust and, with enormous insensitivity, would tell the world her deepest, most intimate thoughts.

These secrets of Mrs. Kennedy were supposed to appear in the book that Harper & Row would publish in three months, and the book was to be preceded by a serialization in *Look* magazine in just four weeks. For the last few months, in fact, the publishing world, which is seldom given to understatement in things, had been awash with rumors that were extravagant even for *it*. What was Jackie *really* worried about? What was Bobby *really* worried about? What was *really* happening?

Some of the rumors were true; most were not. It was said

that Manchester had cracked up; so had an editor from *Look*. Reduced in mind and body by pressure from the Kennedys, the author had fled to a Swiss sanitarium. (The editor from *Look* was toughing it out under the care of three American doctors.) Jackie would sue; Jackie would not sue. A member of the Cabinet had told Manchester that he once thought Lyndon Johnson had ordered the assassination. Robert Kennedy knew the book would damage, perhaps end, his Presidential ambitions. The book reflected on Jackie's sexual problems. Joseph P. Kennedy, in a last hurrah, wanted to smite Harper & Row and *Look* with financial difficulties. The Kennedy family had offered Harper & Row three million dollars not to publish. Jackie herself had offered *Look* one million dollars. Lyndon Johnson was unhappy because *The Death of a President* showed him to be a boor. Lyndon Johnson was happy because it showed the Kennedys to be boors.

It was a splendid collection of rumors, touching on two Presidencies and possibly a third. Furthermore, it involved Jacqueline Kennedy, probably the best-known woman in the world, and it seemed to join her in battle with Harper & Row, an esteemed 150-year-old publishing house, and Cowles Communications, a formidable concern which, besides publishing *Look* and four other magazines, owns newspapers and radio and television stations across the country. Almost forgotten was William Manchester, who did, after all, write the book.

Now, aboard the *Queen Mary*, Manchester had every right not to speak to me, and I had every right to pursue him. There is a style and a ritual in this, and Manchester, who was once a reporter, knew about it. He had traveled from London alone, and that morning he had risen long before dawn to be one of the first passengers to present himself to the immigration officers, who had come aboard and set themselves up in a lounge. Then he had withdrawn to his cabin, retreating to another lounge after the Cunard official had spoken to him. He sat there alone, wrapped in a trench coat, his baggage at his feet, sunken in fatigue.

In repose, Manchester looked a little like Hubert Humphrey. There was the same high forehead and thinning hair, and at the eyes, a little hooded, almost straight across on the lower lids, the corners rose into shallow circles. Manchester is a big man, and in a belted trench coat at dawn after an Atlantic crossing he ought to have looked dashing, like John Wayne. Only he did not. The circles of his eyes had flattened themselves and the lids had drooped and the hooded effect was too pronounced.

He had been ill in London with a fever of 104 degrees; there had been a painful rupture between Harper & Row and himself; he had rejected an earnest, handwritten plea from Jackie Kennedy to revise his manuscript. "I have reached the point where, if the integrity of my manuscript is violated, I have no wish to go on living," he had written to his agent in New York. "It sounds vainglorious, I know, but I am ready to die for this book."

In time, amid a great glare of publicity, Jackie Kennedy did force some changes in the book. But Camelot was to collapse, and a poll was to show that Jackie Kennedy, who once had received about as much public censure as Kate Smith, was "thought less" of by one in every three Americans. More important, Robert F. Kennedy, probably the most interesting figure in American politics, was to complicate his career in spectacular fashion, resurrecting old tales of both his arrogance and his hostility toward Lyndon Johnson.

These things came to pass in the few weeks after Manchester's arrival on the *Queen Mary*, where he sat that morning on a plastic sofa, immobile, pretending to doze. I introduced myself and he repeated what he had told the man from Cunard. He added that he was "out of touch with things," that he didn't know what had started the rumors although he was disturbed by them, and that he was interested only in finishing his book on the Krupps of Germany. Manchester did not know it then, but the attorneys for Mrs. Kennedy had already prepared the legal papers that would draw him into a suit. He did not know about it, in fact, until he read about it the next day in the papers.

It had all begun for William Manchester at precisely nine twenty on the morning of February 5, 1964, when the phone rang in his office on the second floor of the Wesleyan University library in Middletown, Connecticut. He was out and his secretary noted only that a Mr. Salinger had called and that he would call again. "I thought it was Jerry Salinger," Manchester said later. "I hadn't seen Pierre in eight months." Manchester was working part-time as the managing editor of the Wesleyan University Press and writing about the Krupps, a subject that first interested him when he read the Nuremberg trial records. He had tacked three maps of Germany over his long, uncluttered desk and he was in the habit of glancing at them from time to time while he worked, taking concise notes and then stuffing memos into a cluster of Manila folders.

Manchester had arriver at Wesleyan nine years before and he had stayed on because he liked it. A few years before he had been a senior fellow at Wesleyan's Center for Advanced Studies; the Center, while not as eminent a place as Robert Oppenheimer's Institute for Advanced Study at Princeton, but certainly cozier, was becoming a way station for eastern intellectuals.

Manchester lived in Middletown in a house with a fine Federalist doorway. Most of the house had been built in

1790; the rest, a jumble of rooms and a steep stairway, had been tacked on much later. Inside the house there was the debris of children and books, all the dishevelment that accompanies a writer with no particular desire to keep up appearances.

Besides the house, a wife, three children, a green sports car and a dirty station wagon, Manchester had a small, but real, reputation as a writer and reporter. He had been a foreign correspondent for the Baltimore *Sun* and it had left him with a bagful of memories. He had interviewed Churchill and Adlai Stevenson, the presidents of Vietnam and Egypt, and the prime ministers of Burma and Pakistan. Once, in Thailand, he had stood outside the hotel suite of the exiled king of Cambodia while the Thai police, their guns at his midsection, said he could not interview the king because it might offend the French.

Since then he had written four novels, none of which had been best sellers, but all of which had been done in a vigorous, sometimes gamy prose, as well as books about the Rockefeller family, H. L. Mencken, and John F. Kennedy. After the book about Mencken was published, his picture had even been on the cover of *The Saturday Review*. He was, therefore, at forty-two years of age, if not famous, at least mildly renowned in letters, and J. D. Salinger might very well have called him more readily than Pierre might.

The morning of the phone call, Manchester stepped into his office, picked up his secretary's note, and asked where the call had come from. Then he telephoned the White House. Salinger, once the press secretary to John Kennedy, was working for a new President, but as did all the old New Frontiersmen he still retained a loyalty to the Kennedy family. He had called, he told Manchester, because Mrs. Kennedy believed there should be one complete and undistorted account of the assassination and she wanted Manchester to do it.

"I was surprised, of course," Manchester said later, "and I told Pierre that I would think it over. I turned to my secretary and I said, 'Mrs. Kennedy wants me to write the story of the assassination. How can I say no to Mrs. Kennedy?' and my secretary said, 'You can't,' and that's how I first got involved in the project." The next day he wrote to Salinger and asked that he arrange a meeting with Attorney General Robert F. Kennedy. Already he had begun to think about the story.

Salinger did not mention it, but Manchester was not the first author approached by the Kennedys. Theodore S. White, who wrote *The Making of a President,* the celebrated account of the 1960 campaign, was their first choice, and White, although he was close to the family, had declined. Later he said there were no preconditions set for the book when he had been asked to do it, and that he had declined because he knew there would be too much agony involved. He had just written a piece about the assassination for *Life* and it had filled him with horror.

Then the Kennedys had sought out Walter Lord, the author of *A Night to Remember,* the story of the sinking of the *Titanic,* and *Day of Infamy,* a reconstruction of the attack on Pearl Harbor. Lord recalls that Edwin O. Guthman, the press secretary for Attorney General Robert Kennedy, had called and asked him if he were interested. Lord says his first reaction was that he was not, but that he told Guthman he would think it over. He was not called again.

Manchester was the third choice. He was told that the Kennedys were being besieged by requests for interviews from authors who wanted to write about the assassination. The Kennedys knew there would be books written about it, and they wanted to spare themselves the ordeal of treating with so many writers. They would have preferred that no book be written at all, but if one must be done then it ought to be done with the utmost accuracy and good taste. Above all, Robert Kennedy said, the family wanted to avoid sensationalism and commercialism.

These are understandable aims, but to ensure them the Kennedys had to authorize a book and to enter into an agreement in which they would have the right to approve the manuscript before it was published. In return, they would give the author and no one else their cooperation while he was preparing it. Now, politicians authorize their biographies when they are in search of greater office. Movie stars authorize their life stories for their own greater glory. Kings, emperors, and captains of industry have done it for years. All they demand of the author is patience, pliancy, and a certain amount of skill.

The Manchester project, however, was to be on a higher level. It was to be history, even though the phrase "authorized history" has an unfortunate sound, suggesting that the published work will be either trivial or leaden, probably both. Usually it is. Nevertheless, the decision to call for an authorized history of the assassination has been defended by John Kenneth Galbraith and Arthur Schlesinger, Jr., both Kennedy partisans, of course, but both men of parts, as well as academics who know something about history.

Galbraith, author of *The Affluent Society, The Liberal Hour,* and other books, Paul M. Warburg Professor of Economics at Harvard, and a former Ambassador to India, has insisted that the alternative to an authorized history was to have Jacqueline Kennedy write the story herself, or else to open the memories and papers of everyone who was connected with President Kennedy to all authors, or else to maintain a silence on the assassination. The first, he says, was unthinkable, the second impractical, and the third unimaginative.

Schlesinger, a Pulitzer Prize winner in both history and

biography, has defended the decision in similar terms. Still, there is another view. "Those of us who write of public affairs would do almost anything rather than sign such a contract," Theodore S. White said. An authorized history seldom lends itself to either objective reporting or incisive writing. Those who are being written about must have the same picture of life and of history as the author. Bill Manchester was ill-matched with Jacqueline Kennedy and Robert Kennedy. In a particularly infelicitous phrase, she once wrote that she had "hired" him to write the book. He called the book a "sacred trust" and said that he would die for it.

But why Manchester? John Kennedy had read *Portrait of a President,* the book Manchester wrote about him in 1962, and he liked it. Mrs. Kennedy had read one part of a three-part serialization of the book that appeared in *Holiday* magazine. Apparently she liked that, too. Furthermore, Manchester had been the most cooperative of authors when he wrote *Portrait of a President.*

When the Kennedys were in search of an author, it was Salinger who first commended Manchester to them. It is almost mandatory to describe Salinger as portly and cigar-smoking, and to forget that he is tough and shrewd. Salinger was an enterprising reporter for the San Francisco *Chronicle,* who wrote an exposé that led to a tightening of bail bond regulations in California. He joined the staff of *Collier's* and collected information on corruption among the Teamsters. Then he went to Washington to coordinate the release of his information with the opening of hearings by a Senate subcommittee on the Teamsters. Subsequently, *Collier's* folded, but Salinger had met Bobby Kennedy and he was enlisted as a member of the subcommittee staff.

Salinger's first contact with Manchester came in the spring of 1961, when he was press secretary to President Kennedy, and the author sought his aid on *Portrait of a President.* Manchester wrote him that he had never before reported on the Presidency and that he felt what was, he imagined, "a customary sense of awe. I should be eager to have you review the facts in the completed articles," he said. He also said that he would not quote people in the White House unless he had their permission.

Later, Manchester did interview the President. (Manchester recalls that he spoke to him several times; Mrs. Kennedy says he saw him only once. It is one of their smaller disagreements.) The author says he had a genuine empathy with the President, and most likely he did. Manchester was only thirty-nine years old; Kennedy was forty-four. Both men had been born in Massachusetts, both had been in World War II, and both had received Purple Hearts. In fact, when Manchester was a marine on Guadalcanal, John Kennedy was the skipper of PT-109, only a few miles away, across the strait at Tulagi. Almost certainly there were recollections they could share.

In one long discussion, Manchester recalls, they talked about contemporary history. "John Kennedy agreed," he says, "that a reporter was a contemporary historian and that he had to tell a story as straight as he could."

Despite this, Manchester volunteered extraordinary controls on his manuscript to the White House. He told Little, Brown, his publisher, to send the page proofs of the book directly to Pierre Salinger, and he told his agent, the Harold Matson Company, not to release a word of the book for newspaper syndication until the President himself had approved it.

Little, Brown sent the page proofs to the White House, and when they were returned even the typographical errors had been corrected. More important, President Kennedy, or whoever read the proofs, wanted only three words cut from the text. There were no other objections, and the three words,

Manchester says, did not affect the substance of the story at all.

It is extraordinary when a man who is the subject of a book can fault only three words in the manuscript, even when it is extended to him for review. Manchester firmly believes it was because John Kennedy believed in history with the warts on and because he had a deep and abiding respect for the reporter as a historian. There is another view: Many critics thought that the book so relentlessly flattered the President that it was an unrelieved hymn of praise. The book, a reviewer for *The New York Times* said, "can only be described as adoring."

Perhaps the Kennedys ought never to have involved themselves with an authorized history. Jacqueline Kennedy has a formidable sense of privacy; Robert Kennedy has a deep commitment to his political destiny. Neither would ever believe in history with the warts on, and in time, they were to object to several books about President Kennedy and the family. Still, in early 1964 none of these had been written. Indeed, in early 1964 it was probably inconceivable to them that anyone they had actually asked to write a book about the assassination could write something they considered objectionable. Manchester least of all. He had, Salinger remembered, proved his fidelity.

Moreover, Manchester was plainly eager to write about the assassination, and in that first week of February he asked for and received a leave of absence from Wesleyan. Later that month he went to Washington to meet with Robert Kennedy, who said that no one ought to make a great deal of money by exploiting his brother's death. Manchester, in turn, said that he could not bargain over a national tragedy and that he did not want to make a great deal of money. In all things, he said, he would be guided by the wishes of the Attorney General and Mrs. Kennedy. The next day Salinger told him that he would draw up a memo of understanding and that a draft would be sent to him soon. Manchester left then for Middletown; his great work had begun.

Manchester is a compulsive worker and a researcher with enormous tenacity. He was dealing now with the single most electrifying story of his generation. He thought that he would begin his book with a prologue—the dinner the White House held on November 20, 1963, for the Supreme Court—which would be followed by the events of the next five days, and then an epilogue. He read accounts of the assassination, studied them, and drew up lists of the people he would talk to, the places he would visit, the documents he would read. Soon he had a list of two hundred sources that filled five pages of notes.

He had not, however, heard from Pierre Salinger about the memorandum of understanding, and so on March 9, two weeks after their meeting, he wrote to Robert Kennedy and said he appreciated, was, in fact, awed by the demands made on his time, but that he would be grateful for some further indication of what was expected of him. He said he understood that Mrs. Kennedy was eager to get her interviews over with and he said he was ready to leave Middletown on a few hours' notice to see her in Washington.

Then he wrote:

> As for the memorandum—I believe we are in absolute accord there. I agree that it is important that Mrs. Kennedy and you should review the manuscript. If you had not suggested this, I would have. I also agree that no film should ever be made from the book. That would be unthinkable.
>
> That leaves (of the matters that have been raised with me) only the question of publication time. I suggest the memorandum stipulate that the book may not appear before three years have lapsed—say, before November 22, 1966. But that is only a suggestion. If you prefer five years, then five

years it shall be. I have complete faith in your good judgment. My sole concern is that the book be right when it
does appear; that it be a genuine contribution to history.
Anything less simply would not do—for me, as for you.

Manchester enclosed with the letter a eulogy he had delivered on John Kennedy shortly after the assassination. It
had been given, he said, along with thousands of others across
the country in the dark time after the President's death and
"like all the others was totally inadequate. My only excuse
for sending it," he told Robert Kennedy, "is that I would like
you to have it."

He heard from him shortly afterward and two weeks later,
on March 26, both men signed their memorandum of understanding.

As in nearly all things in the dispute that was to follow,
the memorandum itself is wrapped in some haze. Salinger
was to draw it up, but he left the White House on March
19 for California, where he filed his candidacy for the United
States Senate. Salinger left in great haste; it was said that
even President Johnson had only a few hours' notice of his
departure, and the press secretary left some unfinished business. Salinger thinks that a lawyer designated by Harper &
Row drew up the memorandum of agreement. Manchester
says that he himself prepared it and that it was modified in
the course of a day's discussions. Others say it was drawn up
by Robert Kennedy and Ed Guthman, his press secretary.
Most likely it was the work of many hands.

Indisputably, however, Manchester did arrive in Washington on an appointed day and he did call Salinger, who, he
discovered, had fled to California. A day or so later, after
Manchester had hastily rented an apartment in the capital
for $125 a month, Guthman called him, said that he had just
learned of the arrangement for the book, and invited him

over to the Justice Department for a discussion. Evan Thomas, chairman of the Harper & Row editorial board, was there, too.

Before leaving Washington, Salinger had called Thomas and told him that the Kennedys wanted him to work on the book and that they wanted Harper & Row to publish it. Manchester had received a gracefully worded letter from Little, Brown, his regular publisher, releasing him from his commitment to them, and he was free to sign a contract with Harper & Row. Thomas, however, was reluctant. He says he told Salinger that Harper & Row did not want to commercialize the death of President Kennedy and that it would publish the book only if this were agreed. Fine, said Salinger, and Thomas was on his way to Washington.

Thomas, a son of Norman Thomas, the Socialist leader, was an obvious choice for the Kennedys. So was Harper & Row. Ultimately, the battle of the book involved only old friends and neighbors, which was inevitable since only old friends and neighbors were ever invited to participate. Thomas qualified because he had edited and Harper & Row had published *Profiles in Courage,* which John Kennedy wrote in 1955 and for which he won the Pulitzer Prize for biography in 1957.

The book told of brave Senators, and Kennedy put it together while he was recuperating from a dreadful operation on his back. (Kennedy was helped by Theodore C. Sorensen, the Nebraska lawyer who was his chief assistant; Sorensen, too, got involved in the fight over *The Death of a President.*) *Profiles in Courage* lifted Kennedy into a special category, that of a scholarly politician, and it lifted Evan Thomas into a special category, that of literary adviser to the Kennedys.

When Robert Kennedy wrote *The Enemy Within,* a study of union corruption, Thomas edited it, and Harper & Row was again the publisher. Kennedy was helped generously in the writing by John Seigenthaler, his special assistant in the Justice Department, and Seigenthaler and Thomas, in turn, became friendly. (The friendship eventually dissolved; Seigenthaler plunged deep into the battle over *The Death of a President*.) For a while, in fact, if someone in the Kennedy entourage knew that Harper & Row was trying to attract a certain author, he might call the author and say that Evan Thomas was a good guy and why didn't he give him a call.

There were other connections between the Kennedys and Harper & Row, too. Cass Canfield, the head of the publishing house, was genuinely fond of Mrs. Kennedy. His stepson, Michael T. Canfield, had been married to Mrs. Kennedy's sister, Lee Bouvier, and although the marriage ended in divorce the elder Canfield had retained his ties to the Kennedys. (It is possible to take these things too seriously, but there are levels of society at which everyone really does know everyone else: Lee Bouvier is now married to Prince Stanislas Radziwill, who was once married to Grace Kolin, a Yugoslavian shipping heiress, who later married the Earl of Dudley, who was once married to Laura Charteris, who married Michael T. Canfield, who was once married to Lee Bouvier.)

Furthermore, after the death of John Kennedy, Harper & Row had published *The Burden and the Glory*, a collection of his papers, and a substantial part of the profits was given to the Kennedy Library in Cambridge. The publishing house also put out a memorial edition of *Profiles in Courage* for which Robert Kennedy wrote a special preface, and the profit from that was used to establish a John F. Kennedy memorial award for nonfiction writers.

So, on March 25, 1964, when the serious discussions began on this new project, there was the immense advantage of having people who knew each other, who shared an admiration for the Kennedys, and who had been touched with honest grief when John Kennedy died. It ought to have been an auspicious beginning; it was not.

That day, while Guthman wandered in and out, Manchester, Thomas, Kennedy, and Don Congdon, Manchester's agent, met in the Attorney General's office in the Justice Department. It is an impressive office, all dark wood with a fireplace and a vaulted ceiling, murals, a scattering of chairs and a sofa. Kennedy, in shirtsleeves, sat behind an immense desk and repeated what he had said before: he did not went anyone to commercialize his brother's death; the book must be done with taste, dignity, and accuracy. The memorandum was weighed and revised. Only Congdon argued against it. It would, he said, deny Manchester the money to which he would be entitled for such an immense project; he did not think it was fair.

The Harold Matson Company, of which Congdon was a part, has handled a number of well-known writers, and Congdon, a silver-haired, pleasantly hip man, is sophisticated and knowledgeable about the labyrinthine world of publishers and authors. His commitment was to his client; he wanted to make the best deal possible for him. (Later, when nearly everyone was annoyed at everyone else, no one was annoyed at Congdon. From the start he had wisely elected to keep Manchester's interests in mind to the exclusion of all else.)

Manchester, however, turned aside considerations of money. Puffing earnestly on his pipe, he said again that he would not bargain over a national tragedy. He would be proud, he said, if he could contribute to the Kennedy Library. A book about the death of John Kennedy he regarded as a sacred trust. Thomas was emphatic, too, saying that Harper & Row would get a minimal profit of perhaps $35,000 from publication of the hardcover book, far below what it could make if it were a normal commercial undertaking.

In all this there was the honest glow of good fellowship and dedication. John Kennedy had died four months before, but he hovered over that meeting and touched everything about it. Moreover, there was an enormous excitement about being involved with the Kennedys. They are winners, and their exuberance is contagious. They are also glamorous and powerful, and they demand and receive absolute loyalty. Indeed, they must if they are to stay intact.

One truth that emerged from the great book dispute is that the Kennedys are really not very good in dealing with people who have other commitments; they are, in fact, vulnerable to them. No one in the controversy over *The Death of a President* behaved very sensibly or very well, but it was the Kennedys, supposedly ruthless and invincible, who lost the most.

So, with only Congdon registering any dissent, the memorandum was signed by Bill Manchester and Robert Kennedy, seven times on seven copies. Manchester asked for one of the seven, but never got it. Later a Xerox copy was mailed to him.

The heart of the memorandum said that Mrs. John F. Kennedy and Robert F. Kennedy were to review the final text of the manuscript before it was published, and that it could not be published before November 22, 1968, exactly five years after the assassination, unless Mrs. Kennedy decided on an earlier date. It all seemed quite clear, and it said in its entirety:

> 1. William Manchester shall prepare for publication an historical account of the events of and surrounding the death of President John F. Kennedy on November 22, 1963.
> 2. Tentatively, the book will cover the period November 20–25, with an epilogue describing later, relevant events.
> 3. The completed manuscript shall be reviewed by Mrs. John F. Kennedy and Robert F. Kennedy, and the final text

shall not be published unless and until approved by them.

4. No motion picture or TV adaptation shall ever be made based on the book. Other rights may be disposed of by William Manchester, with the approval of Mrs. John F. Kennedy and Robert F. Kennedy, though it is not the intention to prevent the sale of serial option rights to a responsible publisher.

5. At the request of the Kennedy family, the publisher will be Harper & Row. With that understanding, William Manchester has secured a written release from an option held by his present publisher, Little, Brown and Company.

6. The book may not be published before November 22, 1968, unless Mrs. Kennedy designates a prior date, and shall be published at such date thereafter as shall be mutually agreeable to the contracting parties. It is understood that publication will take place promptly after November 22, 1968, unless there is some serious reason for either party to withhold his agreement thereto.

7. Since this account is to be an authorized version, the principle of exclusivity shall prevail until November 22, 1968. That is, members of the Kennedy family shall not cooperate with any other author who wishes to deal with the subject.

8. It is understood that William Manchester may need introductions to certain officials and access to certain pertinent documents. In this matter, Robert F. Kennedy will provide any assistance which he deems wise, and William Manchester undertakes to treat such material with discretion.

9. Upon the signing of this memorandum, a brief public announcement of the project shall be made by Robert F. Kennedy, or by Mrs. John F. Kennedy and Robert F. Kennedy jointly.

10. In the event Mr. Manchester is unable to complete the manuscript or if he should die before completion, Mrs. Kennedy and Robert F. Kennedy will have the right to approve the individual who will complete the work.

11. If both Mrs. John F. Kennedy and Robert F. Kennedy become unable to review the completed manuscript and give

final approval thereto, such approval shall be given by Senator Edward F. Kennedy or someone he designates.

Signed: March 26, 1964

ROBERT F. KENNEDY
WILLIAM MANCHESTER

The signed memorandum shows revisions in Robert Kennedy's cramped handwriting. Where it had said in paragraph three that "the final text shall be approved" by Jacqueline and Robert Kennedy, Kennedy scratched the words out and wrote that "the final text shall not be published unless and until approved by them." In the sixth paragraph, where it had said that the book could not be published before November 22, 1968, Kennedy added the words "unless Mrs. Kennedy designates a prior date."

Manchester had come to the meeting equipped with a version of a suggested memorandum of understanding that he had drawn up on a sheet of copy paper. It was not significantly different from the version he and Robert Kennedy ultimately signed except for his third paragraph, which said:

"3. The completed manuscript shall be reviewed by Mrs. John F. Kennedy and Robert F. Kennedy. Should any passage in the text be objectionable to them for reasons of taste or factual accuracy, it shall be rewritten or deleted entirely."

Manchester points to this as proof of his good intentions. Oddly, the final version never mentioned good taste, although Mrs. Kennedy said later that she was bringing suit against Manchester, Harper & Row, and *Look* because she found *The Death of a President* "tasteless and distorted." If Manchester's memorandum had been adopted, almost certainly it would have been cited as a weapon against him.

It had been arranged that the office of the Attorney General would announce the project, and that Manchester would be left to answer questions from the press as he saw fit. Consequently, he asked Kennedy if he would set up a brief meeting with Mrs. Kennedy so that he might have some better idea of what to say. Kennedy said no, that he and Jacqueline Kennedy were to leave immediately on a skiing trip in Sun Valley, Idaho.

That afternoon, at three o'clock, the Attorney General's office announced that the Kennedy family had "authorized William Manchester to write an extensive account describing the events of and surrounding the death of President Kennedy on November 22, 1963.

"Because versions of what occurred November 20–25 already have appeared and because it is understood other articles and books are in the course of being prepared for later publication," the announcement said, "these arrangements were made with Mr. Manchester in the interest of historical accuracy and to prevent distortion and sensationalism."

It went on to say that "this is a long-term project. Publication of the book may not be expected before three to five years."

The next day, *Look* magazine wired Don Congdon to express its interest in the serialization of a book whose publication it could not expect before three to five years. Congdon told *Look* it was being premature. Undeniably there was the beginning of excitement in the publishing world.

Two

----------------〰〰----------------

WHO is Jackie, what is she? When Manchester first saw her in the spring of 1964 she was an exiled queen who had given the nation a stunning performance as a symbol of continuity when the leadership of the Government changed from one man to another. She had stood by Lyndon Johnson's side when he was sworn in as President, she had led a mighty procession of world leaders along a street in Washington and into a cathedral, and she had told some of them later that peace would be the preoccupation of the new President, as it was of the old. She was dignified and composed in all these things, and it was easy to forget that she was also sad and wounded. There was an abstract quality about the death of President Kennedy. In its mindlessness it touched millions of people, but only Mrs. Kennedy knew its horror. A bullet had shattered her husband's skull; she had been drenched in his blood; she had seen bits and pieces of bone and flesh torn from his body. Manchester was to experience this horror vicariously, to identify with it, and to feel pain. As much as anything else, this led to the character of the book and the argument that followed it.

In early April, Manchester wrote a longhand letter to Mrs. Kennedy and suggested that they meet. A few days later, just before noon on April 7, he visited her in her Georgetown home on N Street. Because of her emotional state, she said, she was unable to participate in an interview, and Manchester, a sympathetic man, said he understood. By everyone's recollection, Mrs. Kennedy, even then, made a powerful impression on the author. She was the widow of the man for whom he had enormous admiration; she was torn and distressed. Indeed, Manchester felt what millions of other Americans felt, but with far more intimacy than they could ever experience.

Ever since President Kennedy entered the White House in 1961, and even before that, there had been a mass suspension of dispassionate thinking about his wife. There were those who despised all the rich, Roman Catholic Kennedys, of course, but there were more who were enchanted by them. Whereas Mrs. Roosevelt was called Eleanor by those who ridiculed her, Mrs. Kennedy was called Jackie by those who were entranced by her. Washington, which has dignity and even a sense of excitement about it, has never been noted for sophistication or great gaiety. Social life there, even among the young, was dreary. Jackie helped to change this, if only by being there.

This was a marvelous accomplishment, just as the impact Mrs. Kennedy made on other lands was marvelous. In Paris, she had been a small phenomenon. President Kennedy had gone there for solemn talks with President de Gaulle. Jackie, who had been a student at the Sorbonne in 1950, accompanied him. She had ridden into Paris in a closed Citroën, visited a child-care center, attended official receptions and state dinners, admired Versailles, gone to a museum with André Malraux—and touched off frenzy. During the visit, at a luncheon for the press, Kennedy had solemnly risen and said: "I do not think it altogether inappropriate to introduce myself. I am the man who accompanied Jacqueline Kennedy to Paris, and I have enjoyed it."

It was nearly the same in Vienna. While the President conferred with Premier Khrushchev the crowds had screamed "Jah-kee," and when "Jah-kee" lunched with Mrs. Khrushchev at the Pallavicini Palace a thousand Viennese stood in the cobbled square outside and shouted until Mrs. Khrushchev led Mrs. Kennedy to the window and held her hand aloft. In London, 250,000 persons lined the streets to see the young President and his wife. The next day a cartoon by Vicky in the London *Evening Standard* showed the Statue of Liberty with the face of Jacqueline Kennedy. One hand held the torch of freedom, the other a copy of *Vogue*.

These are not small things that do not help a country; they do. The effect, however, was to cloud other things about Mrs. Kennedy. She never, for example, identified herself with causes. She did pretty much what she wanted to do, and sometimes she was imperious. In the autumn of 1963 she was a guest aboard the yacht of Aristotle Onassis on a cruise through Greek and Turkish waters. Onassis, the enormously wealthy shipping entrepreneur, was once fined seven million dollars by the United States Government for his behavior in a ship sale. When the public started to become ill-tempered about Mrs. Kennedy's cruise, the President phoned her in Morocco and asked her to come home.

When the President of Pakistan gave Mrs. Kennedy an Arabian stallion, she flew it back in an Air Force plane. He also gave her a necklace which, according to some news stories, was worth about $100,000. There is a precedent that demands that gifts from foreign rulers not be kept. A basement in a Government building is stuffed with things that sheiks, emirs, and potentates have bestowed on Government employees. Mrs. Roosevelt gave jewelry from the President of Brazil to a museum. Mrs. Kennedy kept her necklace for herself. When the President of Ecuador and his wife came to Washington on a state visit, he was told that Mrs. Kennedy was too ill to see his wife. Newspapers next day carried pictures of Jackie water-skiing at Hyannisport. It did not improve relations with Ecuador.

After the death of her husband, Mrs. Kennedy was voted $50,000 a year to pay for her secretarial services. Dwight Eisenhower and Harry Truman got $25,000 apiece for the same thing. Mrs. Kennedy, as the widow of a President, got a pension of $10,000 a year. It is estimated that she inherited ten million dollars from the President.

Mrs. Kennedy, like F. Scott Fitzgerald's very rich people, is different from you and me. This is not to say she is better or worse, but her style is her own. As is Robert Kennedy, she is accustomed to people who are discreet and obedient. As does Robert Kennedy, she succeeds in having friends identify with her. Indeed, she is accustomed to that, too. Manchester did succeed in identifying with the Kennedys but in a way totally different from anything they had expected. In the end, it helped to plunge him and his book into trouble.

Shortly before six thirty on the evening of May 4, 1964, less than six months after the assassination, Bill Manchester rang the doorbell of Mrs. Kennedy's home. It was the first of the two interviews he had with her, and he carried with him his German tape recorder. Mrs. Kennedy, in stretch pants and a jersey, sat and faced him alone for the next five hours. Three nights later he returned, and they talked for another five hours until after midnight.

Mrs. Kennedy, Manchester says, asked him but a single question. On that first night she said, "Are you just going to put down all the facts, who ate what for breakfast and all that, or are you going to put yourself in the book, too?"

Manchester said that he couldn't very well keep himself out of the book, and Mrs. Kennedy said, "Good."

Later, most of the changes that Mrs. Kennedy sought in the book and the serialization involved things that she had told Manchester in the interviews. The question, then, is why did she tell him those things? It does not lend itself to an easy answer.

Undeniably, Mrs. Kennedy, if she thought about it at all, believed she could control Manchester's use of anything she said. There was the memorandum of agreement, of course, but more important than that, Mrs. Kennedy is probably not often challenged after she has taken someone into her confidence. Certainly, this gave her a feeling of restraint.

There is something else: For ten hours Manchester led her over a small point in time, a few days in November. Mrs. Kennedy has excellent visual recollection, and she recalled the minutiae of those days and nights. Indeed, she wanted to recall them, worked at recalling them. On the flight from Dallas to Washington she was given a drink: Scotch. She had never drunk it before and she did not like it. When Manchester spoke to her she sipped a Scotch. She still did not like it, and she hardly needed a stimulant. But Scotch, its medicinal taste in her mouth, helped to remind her of just what it was like that day.

The hours she spent with Manchester were incredibly emotional. They had worked out a hand signal that she used when she wanted him to turn off the tape recorder, and she would say, "I don't think this should be on the tape," but she seldom used the signal, and she used it not at all when she spoke of herself.

Bereaved persons sometimes find solace in talking about the things that have been most painful. Sometimes there is a fierce exultation in it. There is nothing odd about an unhappy woman exorcising her feelings in this way. What is more, Mrs. Kennedy found herself talking for history. History ought to give some meaning to her husband's death. History ought to make it less irrational, enshrine it, show it was not just a mindless happening. "He didn't even have the satisfaction of being killed for civil rights," Mrs. Kennedy had told her mother.

Manchester was the historian, and it gave him a dignity and an attraction. Besides, he was a compassionate man. He shared Mrs. Kennedy's grief. He was interested. He had told her that he didn't see how he could keep himself out of the book. "The interview," a friend of Mrs. Kennedy said much later, "was not the wisest thing she's ever done." Still, it could hardly have been other than it was. It is not surprising that she unburdened herself; it may be more surprising that more of Mrs. Kennedy did not find its way into the book.

Manchester insists that he exercised his own censorship on the four audio tapes he made with Mrs. Kennedy and that the most intimate, the most painful things she told him were never used. There was nothing improper in these things, he says, nothing that would damage her. Manchester says he was just using his discretion.

The tapes themselves were to become a bargaining point in the suit, a lever with which one side could extract concessions from the other. Mrs. Kennedy and Robert Kennedy demanded that the author surrender them and any transcripts he made. It was always understood, they said, that the tapes were to be part of the oral history project on the Kennedy Administration and were to be given to the Kennedy Memorial Library. Manchester says he always intended to surrender the tapes, but that there was never an agreement about it.

As in so many things in the disagreement, both sides may have been right.

Richard N. Goodwin, who later acted as an intermediary

between Mrs. Kennedy and *Look* and Harper & Row, says that he once suggested to Manchester that the tapes be sealed for the lifetimes of Mrs. Kennedy and her children. He says that Manchester agreed to this. Arthur Schlesinger, Jr., points out that he was conducting interviews for the oral history project and that he interviewed Mrs. Kennedy on her recollections up until the time of the assassination. He stopped then, he says, at the single most historic episode of the Kennedy years, because he did not want to subject Mrs. Kennedy to unnecessary pain. Manchester, he thought, would tape the part about the assassination and then give it to the library.

Mrs. Kennedy insists that this was her understanding, too, and that this was one reason she talked so freely. Under the terms by which the interviews for the oral history project are conducted, the person interviewed can select the interviewer and designate a time when the tapes should be made public —in fifty, seventy-five, one hundred years. This is supposed to introduce a feeling of freedom by allowing the person being interviewed to fulfill his obligation to history, however he might see it, and at the same time to be assured that his words will not be used against him.

Nine days after his second interview with Mrs. Kennedy, Manchester had the first of two tape-recorded sessions with Robert Kennedy. It took place at Hickory Hill, his home in McLean, Virginia, just across the Potomac from Washington, and it lasted more than four hours, with just the two men present. Manchester did not return to Hickory Hill until more than two years had passed, and when he did it was under far different circumstances.

Meanwhile, Harper & Row had drawn up a contract for Manchester, which he signed on April 24. It provided that the publisher, after it made a modest profit of 6 percent of the net receipts on the first printing of the hardcover edition, would donate the rest of the money to the library. If a book club leased the right to distribute the book to its members, Harper & Row would get a quarter of the proceeds, Manchester a quarter, and the Kennedy Library a half. The same breakdown would apply on a sale to a paperback publisher.

Soon after, Manchester began the longest, the most tedious, the most agonizing job of his life. An office was made available to him in the National Archives Building, a great imposing pile of masonry that has deep within its bowels documents, books, letters, and statistical abstracts that tell of the American people.

In time, some four hundred cubic feet of documents that the Warren Commission had sifted as it weighed the death of President Kennedy were deposited there. Manchester read nearly all of them. He worked those days on the fourth floor of the Archives Building. Evelyn Lincoln, who had been John Kennedy's private secretary, toiled in the room next to his, sorting out the Kennedy papers.

When he began, Manchester visited Bill Moyers, the idealistic young Texan who was as close to Lyndon Johnson as anyone in the White House, and Chief Justice Earl Warren, who was directing the investigation of the assassination. He wanted Moyers to tell Johnson what he was doing, and he made the first of many requests to interview him. He told Warren that he would use the Commission's findings, but that his would be an independent inquiry into a far broader area than a criminal investigation. The Chief Justice, he says, was courteous and cooperative. Later, he allowed Manchester to read all twenty-six volumes of the Warren Report before it was published.

Because Manchester is a diligent researcher, he read the report and the supporting volumes of testimony not once but several times. Now, since the publication of the report, indiscriminate censure has been directed against both the Commission's findings and its techniques, but the fact is that it is rather easy to isolate single statements from the testimony and to use them to undermine the credibility of the report itself. The testimony is a mélange of contradictions; eye-witnesses differed in their recollections and it led the earliest critics of the Warren Report to some startling conclusions. Manchester faced the problem early in his research; it was an enervating job.

On January 12, 1965, Manchester interviewed Robert Kennedy for the second and final time. The part of the interview that he put on tape took place in the Kennedy suite in the Carlyle Hotel in Manhattan. Then the two had dinner at La Caravelle, an East Side restaurant that the Kennedys favor.

When they spoke, Kennedy was no longer Attorney General; he was a United States Senator. He had established himself as a New York resident, brushed aside the accusation that he was an opportunistic carpetbagger, ignored the hostility toward him among some Democrats in the state, and scored a stunning victory over Kenneth J. Keating, an incumbent liberal Republican Senator. Already even sensible men were beginning to wonder if possibly, just possibly, Robert Kennedy could seize the nomination for the Presidency from Lyndon Johnson in 1968.

Over dinner at La Caravelle, Manchester reminded Kennedy that, if the publication date of November 22, 1968, were left unchanged, the serialization of the book would be published during the campaign. It could embarrass him, Manchester said, by appearing to be a special plea for sympathy. He pointed out that other books about the assassination were being prepared and that early publication of his book might prevent the publication of the others. After all, he said, he was doing the one authoritative account and it would be neither sensationalized nor commercialized. Might not it be a good idea if his work came out sooner than had been planned, thereby discouraging other publishers from putting out inferior, gaudier products?

It was a persuasive argument, and Manchester says that Kennedy seemed to accept it. Manchester told Kennedy that he would take full responsibility for the text and disassociate the Kennedy family from any responsibility for it. Shortly afterward, Manchester, who had not yet begun to write, called Mrs. Kennedy and asked her to intercede for him in getting an interview with President Johnson. She promised to help, but it was to no avail. Manchester also asked Mrs. Kennedy to arrange interviews with her sister Lee Radziwill, Mrs. Rose P. Kennedy, and Pat Lawford, John Kennedy's sister. None of these was forthcoming, although he did speak to Rose Kennedy and Pat Lawford on the phone.

The history of Manchester's attempt to interview Lyndon Johnson is long and involved. He says that he approached the President through fourteen persons, including Mrs. Johnson, but that nothing worked. Twice, he says, in May of 1964 and April of 1965, the President agreed to see him. Both times, he says, the offer was withdrawn.

The problem was partially resolved when Johnson agreed to answer written questions. Before that, there had even been a dress rehearsal for an interview in the West Wing of the White House. Jack Valenti, the aide who once said that he slept better at night because Lyndon Johnson was his President, took the role of the President and for three hours Manchester asked questions about the assassination and the transfer of power from one administration to another. The author recalls it as an extraordinary scene, with Valenti occasionally being summoned into Johnson's office by a buzzer on his desk, and then darting back and playing the role of the President again.

In all, Manchester conducted more than a thousand interviews, with persons as dissimilar as John Kenneth Galbraith,

Marguerite Oswald, and Dwight Eisenhower. He met Galbraith at his country cottage in Vermont, stuck at the end of a long and winding road. It was nighttime, and for a while the two men, their wives beside them, parked their cars hubcap to hubcap and talked of John Kennedy in the dark Vermont night. Manchester spoke to Eisenhower at his farm in Gettysburg, Pennsylvania, and Eisenhower told him that his project was commendable and that one like it ought to have been done after the death of Lincoln.

But of all the interviews, it may have been the one with Marguerite Oswald that made the strongest impression on Manchester. Much later, he spoke of the "triviality of the relationships, the ugliness of the events in Dallas. They would hit me most where I least expected it, as with Marguerite Oswald."

Marguerite Oswald told him that her son was not the assassin of the President and that he had, in fact, been a secret Government agent. She has told others the same thing and when she has she has been at once phantasmic and frightening. Much of Dallas is this way. It is not imagined. It is really there. There were those in Dallas who welcomed the death of John Kennedy, who were gleeful about it. Manchester had venerated Kennedy; the glee had a peculiar effect on him.

Still, Manchester is a thorough and patient researcher. He has had a reputation for this since his first days as a reporter on the *Daily Oklahoman* in Oklahoma City, and for weeks he moved through Dallas, sometimes using his tape recorder, more often taking notes in his meticulous handwriting in a spiral notebook.

He flew to Dallas from Fort Worth after examining the hotel room where the President spent the last night of his life. He drove over the route the motorcade took past the Texas School Book Depository. He stood in the sixth-floor window where Lee Oswald had stood, and he sighted an imaginary rifle at a limousine that would have been going down Elm Street into the Stemmons Freeway at just eleven miles an hour. He visited Parkland Hospital, where Kennedy's body had been taken, where a Dallas official had fought to see that it was not flown to Washington, where a mortician had carefully wrapped six rubber bags around the President's shattered head so that it would not stain the pale green satin of the casket. He went to Oswald's shabby rooming house at 1026 North Beckley, sat in the seat he had occupied when he was arrested in the Texas Theatre, and stood precisely where he had been standing when he was shot by Jack Ruby in the basement of Dallas police headquarters. Manchester covered virtually every inch of ground that Oswald, as well as Kennedy, alive and dead, had covered, and he talked to nearly everyone who knew something of that day in November.

Manchester was to write at length about the political and emotional climate of Dallas, of the peculiar hospitality the city has shown to right-wing petulance, and he spoke to H. L. Hunt, the multimillionaire patron of extreme conservatism. He spoke to Major General Edwin A. Walker, who once proselytized troops in the John Birch doctrine, and he read back issues of the Dallas *Morning News* for a full year.

Dallas is not Kennedy country. The fact that Manchester had been authorized to write a book by the Kennedys did not impress many of those to whom he spoke. For some, it increased their hostility. It is difficult to remember now how intense the vilification of John Kennedy had once been. When James H. Meredith tried to integrate the University of Mississippi there were riots. Men died, Federal marshals and Federal troops were called up, and the Mississippi legislature passed a resolution expressing "utter contempt for the Kennedy clan." Other states, it said, should join Mississippi "in ridding this once great nation of ours of the Kennedy family and accompanying evils."

There has always been an element of that hostility in Dallas, and since the assassination it has been mingled with xenophobia. After the death of Kennedy, Dallas was overwhelmed by investigators from official agencies, from American and foreign newspapers, from the amateur underground that believes in conspiracy. Dallas does not like the investigators; few of the investigators like Dallas. There is one witness who shouts obscenities into the phone when he is questioned about that day, another who will talk only for money, another who consistently changes his account of what he saw. Manchester met them all.

Marina Oswald, however, refused to see him. She had testified before the Warren Commission and the Commission, largely because the Chief Justice is a kind man, had treated her gently. Manchester believed, as did many members of the staff of the Commission, that Marina ought to have been asked more penetrating questions and then put through a rigorous cross-examination. But he could not speak to her and so he learned from others of the sour days and nights of Lee Oswald, of the mean lives and destructive relationships, of the mindlessness of all that passed.

Later, Manchester watched the film of John Kennedy's death that was taken by Abraham Zapruder, the Dallas dressmaker who was standing in Dealey Plaza when the President's motorcade passed by. Manchester does not know how often he saw it, perhaps seventy-five, perhaps one hundred times. There is the President sitting upright, waving, then slumping. A fine spray of blood and pieces of skull are thrown into the air in one quick upheaval. It is wrenching to see this once; it is horrifying to see it as many times as Manchester did.

Others who have explored the assassination have been depressed, but for them it has been an avocation, a job, perhaps only a diversion. For Manchester it was a cause and it demanded all he had to give. The attitude of officials who saw the death of John Kennedy as unfortunate only because it happened in Dallas weighed on him. Their hostility weighed on him. The emptiness of things weighed on him.

By the spring of 1965, Manchester was far into the book, and the book was far into him. In Middletown one evening he sat in his home and read a newspaper. His son John asked him the date, and without hesitating he said, "November 22," and continued reading. Perhaps a minute passed before he realized what he had said.

There were more ominous things, too. In the fall, Mrs. Kennedy received a letter from a woman who had been interviewed by Manchester. She thought he had acted oddly. Once, she wrote, he had stepped to a window and peered at a clump of bushes outside. She said Manchester had insisted the bushes were trembling, that there were men hiding there. "I've been followed," he said, "ever since I began this book."

On November 9, 1965, when a power failure blacked out most of the Northeast, Manchester called Arthur Schlesinger and told him that it was a sign, that it was just the way it had been in Saigon before the fall of Dien Bien Phu. He had been there, Manchester said, and he knew.

Thirteen days later, on November 22, two years to the day after the assassination, Manchester sat alone and wrote that "Lee Oswald was killed in the presence of more than 70 uniformed police officers.". . ."This is Camus," he said later. "This is the theater of the absurd. I sat and stared at it. This was just before I went into the hospital."

For weeks Manchester had been tired, had felt incredible exhaustion. He had reached the part in his manuscript that dealt with Oswald, and to write it he had forced himself to re-create in his mind the events of Dallas, to be both observer and participant. This was no abstract history. It was a painful communion. Manchester's nerves were bad. The passages about Oswald were defeating him. He would sit and stare at the manuscript, toying with a pen, unable to do anything. He is a man long accustomed to erratic hours. Now he would get a long night's sleep and awaken exhausted, still unable to write.

Schlesinger had told friends that he feared Manchester was teetering on the edge of a breakdown. He was, but rumors about it outstripped the reality. In Washington there was a story that he had lapsed into catatonic schizophrenia. A friend called and urged him to at least put in an appearance in the capital and dispel the rumor. Manchester said it was not necessary.

On November 26 he entered a hospital in Portland, Connecticut. For twelve days he lay in bed, unable to work, not wanting to work. On the thirteenth day he rose and insinuated himself into a doctor's vacant office. He had his files and a typewriter brought to him. He stayed there for eight weeks, and when he left his manuscript was nearly complete.

Three

O N March 8, 1966, Manchester wrote to Robert Kennedy: "When I awoke this morning I felt as though I had emerged from a long, dark tunnel. For the past six months I've virtually been a hermit." In the past six months Manchester had brought forth a manuscript of 380,000 words, writing and revising and shuffling passages about, and he thought he was finished. He was wrong. Another long dark tunnel lay ahead.

He had heard from Evan Thomas that Jackie Kennedy would not read the book because it would only reawaken agonizing memories for her. Jackie by now had emerged from isolation. She had visited the West Indies and Acapulco, cruised along the Dalmatian coast and ridden with a New Jersey hunt. She had skied and she had danced, and she had been seen about town, usually by *Women's Wear Daily,* which soon said that she was one of the "REALGIRLS— honest, natural, open, de-contrived, de-kooked, delicious, subtle, feminine, young, modern in love with life, knows how to have fun."

Manchester, who had never thought of Mrs. Kennedy in

those terms, wrote to her and said the book was finished, and despite the prediction by Thomas that she would never read it she had replied: "I was very touched to receive your letter and I'm so glad for you that the book is finished. I know and appreciate all that you went through in writing it. After RFK and Evan Thomas have gone over this manuscript I want you to know that I will read it, too, whenever they think I should."

Late in March, Manchester arrived in New York with five copies of the manuscript. He gave Don Congdon one and Evan Thomas another. The others he carried to Robert Kennedy's office on East 45th Street, where he passed them on to Angela Novello, Kennedy's private secretary. In time, it became important whether or not Bobby, titular head of all the Kennedys, was speaking for Jackie. Manchester insists that he was; Jackie insists he was not. Nevertheless, on that afternoon in March, it seemed that he was, and that Manchester needed to get only his approval for the manuscript.

It was festive then. With some ceremony Manchester had deposited the manuscript and then he and Thomas had taken Miss Novello to lunch at Le Valois. Afterward, she and Manchester dropped in at Mrs. Kennedy's office on Park Avenue. Pamela Turnure, Mrs. Kennedy's private secretary, was there, and the three of them, Miss Novello clutching a copy of the manuscript, went over to the Kennedy suite in the Carlyle, where they discussed the manuscript in general and the Senator in particular. In the past week he had marched in the St. Patrick's Day parade (Mrs. Kennedy waited an hour to wave to him), delivered an address in Mississippi (the governor of the state told the people to be calm), and spoken to students in Tuscaloosa, Alabama (they cheered him).

Manchester had to catch a bus back to Middletown at seven o'clock that evening. Miss Turnure left the hotel with him and as they passed through the lobby and out into the street he asked if he should supply Mrs. Kennedy with a copy of the manuscript. Miss Turnure, he says, told him to "work through Bob, who is representing Jackie."

There was the beginning of a problem here, although neither knew it, and the problem grew because the Senator, too, was to be represented. Angie Novello passed the three copies of the manuscript on to him, and several times he began to read one, stopping each time because he found it too painful. Eventually Ethel Kennedy, his wife, read it, the only member of the family who ever acknowledged reading the book. (Stanislas Radziwill, Lee's husband, read it, but the connection is too distant.) The Senator gave the other two copies to Ed Guthman and John Seigenthaler, his old assistants in the Justice Department. Guthman was now the national news editor of the Los Angeles *Times,* Seigenthaler the editor of the Nashville *Tennessean.* Robert Kennedy wanted them to act as his deputies, to read the manuscript and to comment on its suitability.

Kennedy had first enlisted Seigenthaler and Guthman in 1957 when he was chief counsel of the Senate committee that was investigating corruption in the Teamsters. Guthman, a reporter for the Seattle *Times,* and Seigenthaler, a reporter for the *Tennessean,* were doing the same thing. They co-operated with Kennedy, and when he was named Attorney General they were summoned to the Justice Department. Both were close to Bobby. They were competent and energetic men and they had been a part of the big encounters in his life. Seigenthaler had even managed to get himself stretched out cold while he was protecting the Freedom Riders in Alabama.

Shortly thereafter, Richard N. Goodwin enrolled. Goodwin is tall, dark, and rumpled. A group of reporters who did not know Goodwin once saw him board a plane with Kennedy and they fell to speculating who he might be. They decided he was an Italian reporter with a hangover. Nonetheless, he is a man of talent and parts, and as the book dispute unrolled he became a sort of confidential clerk for the Kennedys, touching off a rich debate among his opponents as to what he was really up to. Was he Jackie's Rasputin? Bobby's hatchet man? Was he pursuing a purpose all his own?

Among themselves, the executives of *Look* got to calling their opponents "the Kennedy goon squad," and Goodwin had a special place on the squad. He was all over the place at once, tipping off a reporter here, annoying Evan Thomas there, maddening *Look* in between. Furthermore, he did these things with zest, guile, and a total conviction that his side was right.

Goodwin, summa cum laude from both Tufts University and Harvard Law, was a House investigator, a White House assistant, and a high State Department official before he was thirty-two years old. He had come to Washington in 1958 to be a law clerk to Supreme Court Justice Felix Frankfurter, and Frankfurter had given him an extraordinary introduction to Washington. The Justice was hooked on gossip, not trivia, but rich conversation about great men and great issues, on the level, say, of the Holmes-Laski letters. Goodwin shared the predilection with him.

After Frankfurter retired, Goodwin became an investigator for a House subcommittee that was looking into rigged television quiz shows. He left the subcommittee after writing an article for *Life* magazine about the investigation, and joined the staff of Senator John F. Kennedy, which was just as well since some members of the subcommittee thought his reliance on the pronoun "I" in the magazine article was presumptuous.

When the Senator became President, Goodwin was one of the few people who still called him Jack, and Kennedy came to rely on him for increasingly important jobs. Goodwin was good at them. Early in the Kennedy Administration he worked with Schlesinger and Adolf A. Berle on a special task force for Latin-American affairs. That summer he attended the Punta del Este Conference on Inter-American Affairs in Montevideo, where he was entrapped into a confrontation with Major Che Guevara, the Cuban Communist, at the home of a Brazilian diplomat. Goodwin returned with a Cuban flag, a humidor of Havana cigars, and the bland assurance that he had avoided any substantive discussions with the Major. In the arcane ways of Latin diplomacy, however, the confrontation touched off an upheaval in Argentinian politics and agitated Cuban exiles in the United States.

Soon after, Goodwin was named Deputy Assistant Secretary of State for Inter-American Affairs. He alienated older men in the State Department by his aversion to protocol, but won the respect of Latin diplomats because of his unerring ability to cut through bureaucratic tangles. In an administration of pragmatists, he was better than most at keeping his eye on the ball.

Eventually Goodwin, along with Adlai Stevenson, Schlesinger, and Chester Bowles, was criticized by Barry Goldwater, which was something like fun in those days, as being "soft on Communism." It in no way handicapped his career. The following year Kennedy appointed him to head the international secretariat of the Peace Corps. At his death, Kennedy was preparing to name Goodwin as his special consultant on the arts. After the assassination, Goodwin stayed on at the White House, where he helped to write Lyndon Johnson's inaugural speech, contributed ideas, and did some research. Meanwhile, he kept up his alliance with Bobby Kennedy and even accompanied him on a trip to South America. Just before Goodwin left the White House to be a Senior Fellow at Wesleyan (and Manchester's neighbor), Arthur Krock wrote in *The New York Times* that his "precocity in the social sciences is deemed by his associates to compare with that of the infant Mozart in the field of musical composition."

There is some question about how Goodwin first got involved in *The Death of a President*. Manchester says that Goodwin had heard at a cocktail party in New York that the manuscript was finished and that he approached him later and asked him for a copy. Goodwin says he has a perfectly clear recollection that Manchester showed up unannounced at his home on a spring night and asked him to read it. It is of small importance. Goodwin was admirably qualified as a reader. He had even been interviewed by Manchester when the author was gathering his material.

Goodwin read the manuscript and advised three changes. First, he suggested a new title. Manchester had been calling his book "The Death of Lancer," an allusion to the code name the Secret Service had used for the President. Goodwin said it ought to be called "The Death of a President," a title, he said, far more dignified and meaningful. Then he suggested that Manchester excise one quote by Mrs. Kennedy, which he did, and that he shorten the ending of the book by about five pages, which he also did.

Whatever the thin line that distinguishes Kennedy friends from Kennedy representatives, Goodwin apparently had not crossed it. He was acting then, he says, simply as an interested party, with no other motive than idle curiosity about what Manchester had wrought. He says that privately he was appalled by things in the book, that he thought it was overwritten, and that it was unfair not only to Mrs. Kennedy but also to President Johnson. He did not, however, tell Manchester any of these things. In fact, at a party in May, Manchester says he overheard Goodwin tell Douglass Cater, an assistant to President Johnson, that *The Death of a President* was a great book and that Johnson would have no reason to regret it.

Which may have been true. Nevertheless, the first real murmurs of political discontent were arising over the manuscript. Evan Thomas, who saw himself as both editor and unofficial representative of the Kennedys, found himself in the unhappy position of protecting on the one hand the book, and on the other the family. To Seigenthaler and Guthman he characterized the book as "a mixture of really great and otherwise," and he worried about its putting the Senator in an impossible position, since all the world knew that he had authorized it. Specifically, he brooded about Manchester's portrait of Lyndon Johnson and his determination to tell it all, to get down each grim detail of the President's death.

Thomas is a mild, slender man who flies a plane, lives quietly with his wife and three children in Huntington, Long Island, and keeps a two-thousand-year-old Greek vase next to his desk because he likes it. He had joined Harper & Row in 1945, when he was twenty-five years old, and he had risen. He had worked with the Kennedys and he had edited books. He did not think he was handling something now that could not be handled, and so he simply went to work. In mid-April, while sending Guthman and Seigenthaler photos of his edited pages, he wrote with happy determination that the book still needed "a tougher going over." By then, Seigenthaler had finished his first reading of the manuscript and he had begun to make suggestions, too. Most of them dealt with Lyndon Johnson.

Now it is well to stop and to consider Manchester's treatment of the man who is Bobby Kennedy's Number One rival in the party. Manchester admits that he is man of dislikes. In a letter to Jackie Kennedy that summer, he said that, while writing the book, "though I tried desperately to suppress my bias against a certain eminent statesman who always reminded me of somebody in a Grade D movie on the late show, the prejudice showed through."

Manchester's own portrait of a President, of how he ought to walk, to talk, and to look had been formed indelibly by John Kennedy. Furthermore, Manchester admired eastern graces. Kennedy personified them and Johnson did not. Johnson had personal mannerisms that would not enchant a roomful of Ivy intellectuals. He is a Texan, he is earthy, and he is not popularly identified with great moral issues. In point of fact, however, he has been far more successful than Kennedy in making Congress do things that help the poor and the suffering, but almost miraculously, even while doing these things, he has sometimes looked not like a benefactor but a cardsharp.

Now, Johnson is sensitive to the things people say about him. If Manchester's book, which was authorized by the Kennedy family, contained an unpleasant picture it was not unlikely that Johnson would be offended and might make it difficult for Bobby Kennedy at a national convention. Moreover, if Manchester's book contained an unpleasant picture of nearly anyone it could make it difficult for Bobby. As the heir to all the good things politics can offer a man, Bobby unites his foes. They look for ways to embarrass him.

After the first installment appeared in *Look,* silver-haired, firm-jawed Governor John Connally, who had not come off very well in it, said it was "filled with editorial comment, based on unfounded rumor, distortion and inconsistency.

"The first published installment of the book *The Death of a President,*" he said, "represented as an 'authorized and authentic history,' turns out to be an astonishing propaganda instrument cleverly woven to reflect favorably on those who gave it birth, while rudely discrediting others involved.

... This transparent attempt to dictate history through a captive voice is shocking," the Governor said, and then announced that his hand had been forced, he would break his silence, rip away the scars and, "in the interest of unmanaged history," tell what really happened in Dallas on November 22. Unaccountably he forgot that seven weeks before he had already told *Life* magazine.

On the same day that Connally was fulminating, Governor John J. McKeithen of Louisiana said, "Kennedy is trying to destroy Johnson, and that's what Manchester's book is all about," and Senator John Tower of Texas was calling Manchester just another "knee-jerk, ultra liberal." Dallas, he said, is a nice place.

Seigenthaler, Guthman, and Thomas foresaw things like this, and they knew that even if politics were not involved there was a certain delicacy with which reputable authors and publishing houses treated the President of the United States. Now, the fact is that Manchester's book was never as hostile to Johnson as its detractors said, despite their great hauling out of adjectives and verbs as evidence of Manchester's ill will: When Mrs. Kennedy stumbled into her bedroom on Air Force One she saw Johnson "sprawling" on the bed, dictating a letter. Then he "heaved himself up and hastily lumbered" past her. In the final version, "sprawling" became "reclining." Johnson, however, still heaved and lumbered. Johnson also meets in Fort Worth with his "tong"; two other Texas politicians are stalking each other with "shivs"; Lady Bird "never had much luck with names." There is a great deal of this in *The Death of a President*, but it seems frivolous to say these passages indict Johnson. In another book they would have passed unnoticed.

Far more serious than the adjectives and the adverbs was what became known among early readers of the book as the "deer-hunting incident." Manchester had dropped his earliest idea of beginning the book with the dinner that the White House gave for the Supreme Court and instead had begun with a description of a visit that Kennedy made to the Johnson ranch eight days after the election. Johnson suggested that they go on a deer hunt at dawn, and Kennedy accepted, though he was appalled at the idea of killing an animal. At 6 A.M. they turned out by the ranch house, Johnson in weatherbeaten cowboy clothes, Kennedy in a checked sports jacket and slacks. They left in Johnson's white Cadillac, zooming and jouncing across the fields, and Kennedy was forced to shoot his deer; the Vice-President-elect shot two. The President, Manchester wrote, had been haunted by the recollection of the helpless animal caught in his gunsights. By implication, the Vice-President had enjoyed the whole thing.

Manchester's book, of course, was about an assassination. It told of a man who was killed in the state of Texas by a rifle bullet, and almost certainly the picture of a Vice-President from Texas who hunted things was not the best of all ways to begin.

"The portrait of the Vice-President is fine when it sticks to facts," Arthur Schlesinger wrote to Manchester after he read the manuscript, "but too often it acquires an exaggerated symbolism." Schlesinger added that some critics were almost sure to see Johnson as an expression "of the forces of violence and irrationality which ran rampant through Dallas."

Manchester did take the deer-hunting incident out, prune it a bit, and drop it elsewhere in the book. He agreed that it was the wise thing to do, and he said he had not meant to imply bad things about Johnson. (Later a letter that Manchester sent to Evan Thomas fell into the hands of the Kennedy partisans. "At the same time he agreed with me that it might be inappropriate to open a book about the death of President *Johnson* with a section about Lyndon Johnson," he wrote. Freudian slip, the Kennedy partisans insisted.)

Lost sight of sometimes in the publicity that soon surrounded the dispute was Manchester's treatment of the
Kennedy partisans. Sometimes he had made them look un-
generous, and sometimes he had spoken of the hostility they
felt toward Johnson. This, while proving that an authorized
history cannot be all bad and that Manchester was an honest
man, also gave the politicians something to feed on.

For instance, of the flight from Dallas to Washington
aboard Air Force One, Manchester quoted a Secret Service
man as saying there was "a great deal of tension between the
Kennedy people and the Johnson people." He wrote that Mrs.
Kennedy, as well as Ken O'Donnell and Larry O'Brien, two
of her husband's closest assistants, had refused to sit with
Johnson, that Johnson's secretary had been rebuffed by Kennedy's secretaries when she made a small, human gesture
toward them, and that Kennedy's old assistants declined to
attend the swearing-in of the new President.

The alleged refusal of the assistants to attend the ceremony
became a small controversy in itself after it appeared in *Look*.
Manchester had written that pictures of the swearing-in
showed not a single Kennedy aide there. Shortly after the
Look installment appeared, the Boston *Globe* published an
uncropped photograph of the swearing-in that showed Ken
O'Donnell standing next to Mrs. Kennedy while the oath was
being administered. Moreover, it noted that Manchester had
written that, during the swearing-in, O'Donnell was pacing
a corridor like a caged tiger. It is a point, but it does not
discredit the book. The corridor is next to the stateroom
where Lyndon Johnson became the new President. O'Donnell
might very well have paced there during part of the ceremony. Furthermore, Manchester wrote about an atmosphere
that was charged and full of tension. This was the main point,
and whether or not O'Donnell stepped to Mrs. Kennedy's
side was incidental.

Whatever the state of the manuscript that spring, there seemed to be some agreement that it ought to be published not in 1968, but in the fall of 1966. Thomas had suggested this possibility to Kennedy and had reminded him that a book by Jim Bishop on the assassination was scheduled for the fall. "Oh, my God, yes, that," the Senator said. Thomas, wise in the ways of books, knew that early publication of *The Death of a President* would help it compete with *The Day Kennedy Was Shot*, which, after all, would not be an *authorized* history. Earlier, Bishop had requested help from Mrs. Kennedy in preparing his book. Mrs. Kennedy had denied the request and he had made it a second time. She had written to him:

> So I hired William Manchester to protect President Kennedy and the truth. He was to interrogate everyone who had any connection with those days—and if I decide the book should never be published—then Mr. Manchester will be reimbursed for his time. Or if I decide it should be known—I will decide when it should be published— sometime in the future when the pain is not so fresh. I suppose I must let it—for I have no right to suppress history, which people have a right to know, for reasons of private pain.

After he received the letter and noted that Manchester had been hired, Bishop reportedly said that Mrs. Kennedy "was trying to copyright the assassination," which may have been unjust. Nevertheless, the Kennedys were plainly apprehensive about any book other than Manchester's. At the end of April, Manchester told Don Congdon, his agent, that he had spoken on the phone with Seigenthaler, Thomas, and Guthman and that all were agreed that the book ought to be published in the fall. The following day, still in something approaching high spirits, Manchester called Guthman in Los

Angeles and Guthman said that he had sat up all of one night reading the book and that he would recommend to Mrs. Kennedy that she not read it at all. It would be, he said, too painful.

Jackie Kennedy was in Spain then, visiting with a collection of dukes and duchesses and being bothered by photographers who turned a charity ball she attended into a shambles. She also was touched by rumors: she was romantically interested in the Spanish Ambassador to the Vatican, a sixty-two-year-old widower with eight children; there was a coolness between her and Princess Grace of Monaco. "Silly," said Angier Biddle Duke, the American Ambassador to Spain, to the first. "Nonsense," said Princess Grace to the second. The trip, despite the rumors and the papparazzi, was still something of a success. Jackie Kennedy was photographed on horseback while wearing a dashing Andalusian costume. She had flown a hairdresser from Madrid to Seville before the photographs were taken, and they were stunning.

When Mrs. Kennedy returned in early May, she saw Goodwin in New York, told him that she felt "warmly" toward Manchester, and told Goodwin to tell him that she hoped he would understand if she did not read the book. Manchester, pleased that Mrs. Kennedy was apparently happy, hastened to tell Thomas about the message. Thomas said fine, but his doubts about the book were growing stronger. In publishing, there is, or at least ought to be, a very special relationship between the editor and his author. It is acceptable for an editor to harbor bad thoughts about a book. He may tell his colleagues about it. He may tell his wife about it. He may think the book is a clinker, but there is just so much that he may tell a sensitive author. Accordingly, while Manchester knew that Thomas had some reservations about his manuscript, he was not aware of the depths of Thomas' passion.

On May 16, Thomas wrote to Seigenthaler and Guthman:

I got through what I hope is my last and third reading up to page 606 of the Manchester late yesterday afternoon and sent the attached night letter to Ed [Guthman] (the purpose of this night letter being that I had on Friday very casually thanked Ed for his good notes and written as though I assumed that there would be no further necessity for discussion after John [Seigenthaler] had read this script as edited—whereas, actually I think I'm going to need to not only get both of you to read the edited script, but to give me your professional advice as well as your advice as RFK's representatives). Frankly, gentlemen, I am deeply disturbed by some of this. It's in part, I guess, an ambition to make sure that Bob Kennedy is not hurt by association (an association which he cannot escape) with the book which is, in part, gratuitously and tastelessly insulting to Johnson, and for that matter, the memory of the late President Kennedy, while at the same time being a really considerable piece of work, one might almost say a great book. Then, I have the professional publisher-editor view that it would be a damn shame to not at least do what is humanly possible to make this the great book which it can be.

It's almost as though Manchester had become so deeply involved in this tragic narrative that he could not resist turning it into a magic fairy tale. The marvelous Irish politician who became one of the world's great statesmen is almost deprived of his miraculous self; being seen as the child of Arthur and Guinevere. While Black Jack Bouvier's daughter is somehow deprived of some of her hard-won stature by being born of elves in a fairy glade and dressed in such magic cloth of gold (chosen by Prince Jack) that the Texans in their polka dot dresses and bow ties are seen as newly arrived scum—plucked from the dung heap by magical Jack (it seems to be entirely forgotten that Lyndon Johnson was a very tall Majority Leader of the Senate while John F. Kennedy was very much of a back row young Senator who had not yet been truly inspired toward the path of greatness). And, the palpable fact that the author wants so badly to condemn Oswald as a product of the Dallas-Birch sickness seems to me to *intrude* to the point of suspicion-making.

Thomas went on to offer Guthman and Seigenthaler five hundred dollars apiece because, he said, he was asking them to be "more than just Bob Kennedy's proxies." Guthman and Seigenthaler declined the offer of the five hundred dollars, but they did agree to be more than just Kennedy's proxies. They had been making suggestions for revisions in the book and nearly all the suggestions had dealt with political matters. Thomas was making revisions, too, and so were other editors at Harper & Row. Meanwhile, Manchester, a prodigious re-writer, had some ideas of his own. For example, without much prodding from the other readers, he was now ready to pull the deer-hunting incident away from the front of the book. He had also heard from Arthur Schlesinger, to whom he had sent a copy of the manuscript, and Schlesinger's comments had left him reflective.

Schlesinger sent a long memorandum about the book, offering page citations and general comments, and the thrust of the message was that Manchester had done some things splendidly and some things rather poorly. "The rendition of the flight back to Washington on AF-1, for example, is magnificent," Schlesinger wrote, thereby contradicting what was to be a later consensus among Kennedy advisers.

Schlesinger, a genuine historian, also took issue with some of the editing that had been done by Thomas, Guthman, and Seigenthaler. Several times he wrote, "Restore. Why protect Dallas?" Other times he noted, "Restore the deletions. This is history," or simply, "I don't understand the deletions." He also wrote that he saw no reason to protect J. Edgar Hoover. The director of the Federal Bureau of Investigation did not come off particularly well in Manchester's manuscript. He appeared to be unconcerned when he learned of the President's death, and he showed neither sympathy nor respect for Robert Kennedy's sadness. Moreover, Manchester pointed out that his bureau had known that Oswald, once a defector, was in Dallas, and that Hoover had been furious when the Warren Commission suggested that the bureau had been negligent in not reporting it. Manchester had also quoted, with scathing effect, Sargent Shriver's comments on Hoover's warning that the funeral march along 17th Street to Saint Matthew's Cathedral could be dangerous. Shriver had thought that Hoover was simply protecting himself, preparing a defense of "I told you so" if anything should happen.

Schlesinger may have been kind to Manchester because he believed the author had suffered enough in writing the book, but he was also willing to offer some criticisms. "I think this is a remarkable and potentially a great book," he wrote, but, he said, as had Evan Thomas, Kennedy was portrayed as too much of a "husband, father, the young prince and not the world leader and tough politician." He told Manchester that his "literary gifts" were "essentially in narrative and atmosphere," but that his language was too lush, that it lacked the austerity that a serious work of history should have. "Worse," he wrote, "the narrative is too often interrupted by passages of sententious generalization."

Schlesinger, too, took exception to the description of Johnson. "The portrait of the Vice-President is fine when it sticks to facts, but too often it acquires an exaggerated symbolism," he said. He also found fault with some facets of Manchester's interpretation of the new President. Once he wrote: "JFK regarded LBJ as a valuable piece of Americana. I disagree with the implication of 'enough to fault him in the eyes of the Boston patrician.'" Another time he disagreed with Manchester's description of the political relationship between the then Vice-President and John Kennedy. Schlesinger said that he did not "think that JFK looked to LBJ 'for a strong hand on the Hill.' Indeed," Schlesinger wrote, "he rather kept him out of Congressional matters." A little further on in the memo Schlesinger even noted a little severely that "LBJ has a sense of humor, if of a special sort."

Schlesinger was concerning himself primarily with the author as historian, not as family chronicler of the Kennedys. He congratulated Manchester on "an extraordinary job of research and synthesis," and although he had reservations about Manchester's disclosures about Jackie Kennedy he was not prepared to battle him about them. Among all the readers of the manuscript, in fact, there was a general uneasiness about the way Manchester had handled some personal details about Mrs. Kennedy—her reactions to her husband's death, her behavior at his coffin, the letter she had written to him—and there was even more uneasiness about Manchester's predilection for gore. He had, after all, seen the Zapruder film many times. He had spoken at length to Mrs. Kennedy, who had recalled every last horror, and with great fidelity he had faithfully transcribed her report. Nevertheless, the emphasis in the early weeks of revisions was on the political, not the personal.

Mrs. Kennedy, since passing on a message of affection to Manchester in May, had not been involved in the book at all. By then there was a great criticism of the Warren Commission, both of its conclusions and its techniques, and Mrs. Kennedy and members of her family were publicly ignoring them. Not that she was having much peace. She had returned from Spain and found that her descriptions of bullfights she had seen there as "exciting" and "beautiful" had agitated American animal lovers. Cleveland Amory, speaking for the Humane Society, said it was sad that Mrs. Kennedy had condoned "one of the last relics of the barbarism of the past era."

Then there was some healthy debate among the people who write letters to editors, most of whom agreed with Mr. Amory. A little later, Mrs. Kennedy enrolled in the battle to save the Metropolitan Opera House from the wrecker's ball, but Rudolf Bing, the acerbic manager of the Met, noted that Mrs. Kennedy had "very rarely" attended the Met in the first place and could hardly be expected to know the dishevelment of the building. "I regret," he said, "that such a distinguished lady allows herself to comment on something about which she is so ill-informed." Soon afterward, Mrs. Kennedy and her children left for a vacation in Hawaii. She did not return until the end of July and when she did she plunged the battle of the book into open warfare.

All this time, Evan Thomas was working more with Guthman and Seigenthaler, both of whom had filed long memos about the book, than he was with Manchester. Manchester, growing a trifle nervous about what was happening to his manuscript, wrote to Thomas and asked him what changes were being made. Thomas, growing nervous about his author, tried to soothe him. He also told Seigenthaler that Manchester needed "love and affection," that things were difficult, he knew, but that almost certainly everything would work out. Manchester, who had apparently accepted Goodwin as an official Kennedy adviser by then (Goodwin says he was not), also pressed him for more suggestions about the manuscript. Goodwin was a neighbor. Goodwin was a friend of the Kennedys. Did he think anything further should be done with the manuscript? Whatever his real feelings, Goodwin said no.

The manuscript, it must be remembered, was of terrible importance to Manchester. He had devoted more than two years to it, and he had borne burdens, not just psychological ones, but practical ones as well. For one thing, he was running out of money. Harper & Row had given him an advance

THE MANCHESTER AFFAIR   66

of $40,000 in three parts. The publishing house planned then to put out 45,000 copies of the book, which would cover the advance at a standard royalty rate of 15 percent on the ten-dollar book. (Ultimately, they decided on a first printing of nearly 600,000 copies.) Manchester, who received no financial aid from the Kennedys, although he did get some office space, had nearly exhausted the advance. When he had undertaken the project he had left his part-time job as editor of the Wesleyan University Press, which paid $10,000 a year, rented an apartment in Washington at $125 a month and commuted to his family in Middletown. A few months later he had moved his family to Washington and taken another apartment for $350 a month. He had traveled much, conducted extensive interviews, and spent money. *Holiday* magazine had asked him to write several articles and he had refused because he was too busy. Another publisher had asked him to write a book it was planning to call "Eisenhower's Generals," and he had declined that, too. Furthermore, he had delayed his own book on the Krupps and had lost his title, "The House of Krupp," when another book used it.

So Manchester was nervous about the book, and he was not enthusiastic about the changes sought by Seigenthaler and Guthman. He was not enthusiastic about any more changes at all, in fact, and when he heard that Pamela Turnure, Mrs. Kennedy's private secretary, wanted a copy of the manuscript he asked Thomas not to give it to her, citing the conversation he had with her a few months before in the Carlyle when she had said that Robert Kennedy would act as Mrs. Kennedy's agent and that it was not necessary that Mrs. Kennedy get a copy. Thomas, however, passed on a copy to Miss Turnure, leaving Manchester a little unhappier than he had been before.

Miss Turnure had figured in a small way the year before in a dispute over a book to which Jackie Kennedy had objected.

It was *White House Nannie,* Maude Shaw's story of "My Years with Caroline and John Jr." Mrs. Kennedy, after learning that the book was to be brought out in England, asked Sol M. Linowitz of the Xerox Corporation to speak to the publisher, Michael Borisson, director of Angley Books and chairman of Southern News Services, Ltd. Borisson recalls that Linowitz visited him in London in September, carrying a copy of the manuscript that he had apparently got from someone in Italy to whom it had been offered for serialization, and immediately raised the threat of an injunction against publication. Borisson says he thought this was silly and that he told Linowitz so. Miss Shaw, he says, "just wanted to write a nice book." Nevertheless, Borisson agreed to visit New York to discuss the book with Mrs. Kennedy. When he arrived, however, he did not see Mrs. Kennedy. He saw instead Miss Turnure, Linowitz, and a man whose name he can't recall, but who, he thinks, was from the Justice Department. Consequently, about a hundred words were deleted from the book, which eventually was published here in April of 1966 by the New American Library after it had been serialized in *The Ladies' Home Journal.* It mentioned that Miss Shaw had told Caroline of her father's death, and it was to this that Mrs. Kennedy objected most strongly. Later she took some pains to have this excised from *The Death of a President,* and she did to a degree succeed.

On June 9 and 10, Thomas and Manchester sat down and reviewed the changes sought by Seigenthaler and Guthman. Miss Turnure had not been heard from yet. Manchester later rewrote a few passages and, he says, "incorporated" the changes. A week later he sent the revised pages to Thomas, but they still left the editor unhappy, and the next day he told the Kennedys so. Consequently, Senator Kennedy ordered a fresh review of the manuscript, and at the end of June, Thomas, Seigenthaler, and Guthman met in the Jefferson Hotel, Washington, for what they called the "marathon editing session." On July 9, Thomas, in one great swoop saw both Seigenthaler in Nashville and Guthman in Los Angeles. It began to look as if the book would indeed be published by the end of the year, and Manchester began to think he was home free.

Four

———————

WHEN Thucydides, the celebrated Greek historian, sat down to begin his history of the Peloponnesian War, he wrote: "The task was a laborious one because eyewitnesses of the same occurrence gave different accounts of them as they remembered, or were interested in the actions of one side or the other." As everyone knows, the history that Thucydides wrote, although it includes some smashing speeches, told mostly of Athenians and Spartans knocking one another off. It was all straightforward stuff about which the participants could disagree on some peripheral things, but not about the big picture. It is not so with the dispute between William Manchester and the Kennedy family. Bobby Kennedy either did or did not give permission for the publication of *The Death of a President*. It all depends on whether the eyewitnesses were interested in the action of one side or the other.

Early in July of 1966 there seemed to be general agreement that a book could be gotten out by the end of the year. The question was what book. Manchester and his agent wanted to submit the manuscript to magazines for bids on the right to serialize it before publication. Manchester, however, had not made all the changes that Seigenthaler and Guthman wanted. Indeed, there seemed to be some shades of difference between the editor of the Nashville *Tennessean* and the national news editor of the Los Angeles *Times* on what the changes ought to be. In one long memo the previous month, Guthman had written that he had "read all and dissented where I thought I should—RFK's interests or not." He also said of the book: "It is a great job and I believe it will be a landmark in the history of the Kennedy era."

In all, Seigenthaler and Guthman had pressed for 111 changes in the manuscript, and Harper & Row had wanted some, too. One problem, however, was: What was a change? Rewriting a section? Excising it entirely? Changing a word here and there? No one seemed to have a very clear idea, and when Manchester said he had "incorporated," not made, the changes, he may have been using the most accurate word he could.

Throughout these months, neither Seigenthaler nor Guthman had any substantive conversations with Manchester although they were helping to edit his book, and most of what they knew about Manchester's state of mind was passed on to them from Thomas. According to Seigenthaler, each time he did talk to the editor from Harper & Row he heard parlous reports about the author. Thomas, he says, was forever telling him that Manchester was ready to jump off a roof if there was no encouragement from the Kennedys. "Evan would say that someone's got to indicate to him that the world's not coming to an end," Seigenthaler declared, "and then he would say, 'There's no question but that he's seen that film seventy-five to one hundred times and if you'd seen the President's brains fly that many times then something would happen to you, too.'" One time that Thomas said that to him was July 14, and on that day the dispute was really born.

To begin with, there were at least two important phone calls made on July 14. Seigenthaler made the first from Nashville—a conference call to Manchester in Middletown and Thomas in New York. Later he called Thomas a second time, and after they had spoken for a while, Thomas told the Harper & Row switchboard to hook Manchester in again from Middletown. There was a period, then, in which Seigenthaler and Thomas spoke alone.

Seigenthaler says that confusion took wing that day, and that no one now really knows who said what to whom. He says that Thomas told him Manchester was unhappy and that a letter or telegram from the Kennedys would reassure him. Manchester recalls that there was indeed talk of a telegram, and that Thomas told him later that Seigenthaler had said it would indicate that the Kennedys had now approved the manuscript for publication. Thomas, in turn, says that Manchester told him that Seigenthaler had said the telegram would indicate that the manuscript had now been approved for publication. He himself, Thomas says, believed the telegram would mean that the book could be published later that year, not in 1968. It is, of course, confusing, and the events of the next few weeks mucked it up even more.

Thomas, confident that all was well, was ready to leave on vacation after the phone calls, but before he did he sent Seigenthaler a draft of a telegram. Seigenthaler was to pass it on to Kennedy, who would read it and then presumably send it to Manchester. Manchester, meanwhile, thinking that things were in the bag, sat down and wrote to Bobby Kennedy:

JULY 17, 1966

DEAR BOB:

Naturally I was pleased to hear from Evan Thomas Thursday that you agree with us about the desirability of publishing the book the first week in January 1967, preceded by the usual serialization, and that you are writing me to that effect. I was especially touched by your reason for approval; President Kennedy's opinion of me and my work. As you know, that is a prize I cherish above all others, and I shall continue to try to be worthy of it.

The book benefited enormously from the suggestions of the five readers: Evan, John Seigenthaler, Ed Guthman, Arthur Schlesinger, and Dick Goodwin. John and Ed were especially generous of their time and perceptive in their comments. Because of them, the manuscript is tighter, stronger, and more responsible. In writing it I attempted to keep a taut rein on my own feelings. Inevitably they sometimes intruded, however, and the readers were, therefore, as invaluable as they were necessary. Of course, Evan and I will continue to scrutinize the text carefully, to make certain that no abridgement violates the version we've all agreed upon.

I'm convinced that our appearance early next year will eliminate most of the problems created by irresponsible books about the tragedy. For example, Epstein's *Inquest,* a really poisonous job, needn't trouble us any longer. With the help of Dr. Burkley and Howard Willens I think I've knocked out what, at first reading, appears to be the one strong point in Epstein's version.

I'm enclosing *Red Roads to Mandalay,* a collection of my dispatches from Hanoi and Saigon which the Baltimore *Sun* published in 1953 on the eve of Dien Bien Phu. I think it shows how little the situation there has changed in the past thirteen years, and what the real stakes there are. It doesn't make for encouraging reading, I'm afraid. But perhaps it's a contribution toward realism.

Faithfully,

WILLIAM MANCHESTER

A few hours after he wrote the letter, Manchester received a call from Seigenthaler, who told him that Joseph P. Kennedy had suffered a heart attack and that the Senator had left Washington and rushed to his side. The telegram, Seigen-thaler said, would be delayed. Manchester says Seigenthaler also reaffirmed that the manuscript was now approved. Sei-genthaler says he did nothing of the kind. Nonetheless, the next day, Don Congdon, Manchester's agent, did pass out copies of the manuscript to six magazines.

In the next few months, after the manuscript had become a very hot item (What did it say? What *is* Jackie really wor-ried about?), there were people all over New York who were absolutely certain that they could get a copy and read it, or who knew people who said they had read it, or who knew people who knew people who said they had read it. Accord-ing to the conventional wisdom, office boys in the six maga-zine offices had worked by night and run off copies of the 1,200-page manuscript on Xerox machines, and then sold them, presumably to other office boys with other Xerox machines. The fact is there were a few copies around, but never as many as the insiders thought. One author, for reasons all his own, compounded the confusion by composing a full-length manuscript about the assassination. When he was finished he wrote "The Death of a President" on the title page.

Congdon, however, had sent only seven Thermofax copies of the manuscript to six magazines—*Look, Life, The Saturday Evening Post, The Ladies' Home Journal, McCall's,* and *Good Housekeeping. Life* got the extra copy. An editor was recuperating from an illness and wanted to read it at home. *Time* magazine reported later that Congdon had also sent a copy to United Artists, despite the ban in the memorandum of understanding on film sales. It was not true. Congdon had dealt only with the six magazines.

With each copy of the manuscript, Congdon passed on a letter in which he asked each editor to treat his copy with discretion. He asked them to guard against news leaks and he asked that they not make the manuscript freely available to members of their staffs unless it was absolutely necessary. This, however, was not done and at least one other magazine and one book club received copies of the manuscript, presumably from one of the original six magazines. "Magazines," Congdon said later in disgust, "are not what they used to be. In the old days things like that never happened."

The first person to see the manuscript at *Look* was William B. Arthur, the editor, who immediately gave it to Mike Land, a senior editor. Land, a slender, buoyant, dark-haired man, ponders the merits of as many as a thousand books a year for *Look*. He passes a great many of them on to other editors who might be expected to know something about their subjects, but *The Death of a President* he would read himself.

Land, in fact, was a particularly suitable man to read it. Nearly everyone who got involved with *The Death of a President* had some connection with someone else, and Land had helped Paul B. Fay, the former Under Secretary of the Navy, write his recollections of John Kennedy. The book was called *The Pleasure of His Company,* and when it was published the critics said that it was just a light-hearted memoir. (Mrs. Kennedy deputized John Kenneth Galbraith to read that one.) Nonetheless, both Jacqueline and Robert Kennedy had objected to it. Robert Kennedy thought that Fay had treated Joseph Kennedy irreverently. Mrs. Kennedy thought that Fay had taken advantage of his friendship with the President by publishing the book. When he gave her a check for $3,000 for the Kennedy Memorial Library she rejected it.

Land took about six hundred pages of the manuscript to his home in New Rochelle that night. He read it and was hooked. The next morning the first *Look* executive he saw in the office was Bob Meskill, one of two managing editors.

"Bob," he said, "I'm afraid we've got a great book on our hands." Land handed the six hundred pages on to Bill Arthur, the editor, who began reading it in his office. It gripped him, too.

Each of the seven copies that Congdon had sent out showed passages that had been deleted with great, dark strokes, making it impossible to read what was beneath the strokes. Each deletion had been initialed: "JS" for John Seigenthaler, "EG" for Ed Guthman. Perhaps the editing slashes, confirmation that the manuscript had been worked over, helped to heighten everyone's interest. Certainly there was enthusiasm for *The Death of a President* at *Look.* Arthur read the book that day in sections, and then passed it in, piece by piece, to Gardner Cowles, the chairman of Cowles Communications. He liked it, too. That night Land took home the second part of the manuscript, and when he returned the next day there was the first of a week-long series of editorial conferences about the manuscript.

That same day, according to Manchester, Seigenthaler again spoke to Thomas and again he said the manuscript was acceptable to Robert Kennedy. Manchester says Thomas told him so. Whatever was really happening will probably be buried forever. Nonetheless, there are little bits and pieces of evidence that were collected later by the lawyers in the dispute. For example, Angie Novello, who has been Kennedy's private secretary since he was battling the Teamsters in 1957, keeps daily message sheets of all incoming telephone calls to Kennedy's office. She is also a prolific writer of memorandums. On July 21 she wrote to the Senator:

> Bill Manchester called. He's quite worried about that letter you're supposed to send him. John [Seigenthaler] told him that you were going to send it and that he was going to talk to you about it, but he hasn't heard a word from John. Copies of the manuscript are in the hands of some

magazines and since he wants to protect you and the family he should have the letter in his possession.

A few days later she wrote:

> John Seigenthaler called a few minutes after you left the office and dictated the following letter which he said Evan Thomas wanted for Bill Manchester. It's very rough and you will no doubt want to change it but he and Ed will discuss it with you in the morning.

Miss Novello insists the telegram was sent later only to make it clear that Kennedy was not opposed to the serialization or the publication of the book after its text was approved. She also says she was told repeatedly that the author was worried and concerned over his work. Both Manchester and Thomas, she says, seemed eager to hear that Kennedy would not stand in the way of the sale of serial rights.

On July 27 she wrote: "Evan Thomas called. . . . He also wanted to know if you've done anything about that letter for the magazine publishers on Bill Manchester's book."

Thomas seemed to have a sort of premonition about the telegram. Sometime between July 26 and July 28, Miss Novello recalls, he called her and suggested that Senator Kennedy, rather than sending the telegram to Manchester, send it to him. Thomas said that he would keep it in his safe and that it would be used only when he thought it appropriate. He said that if Manchester needed it to prove to the magazines that the Kennedys were willing to permit serialization, he would furnish him with a copy.

Others besides Thomas were impressed that the situation demanded delicate handling, that it was not just another book that was under discussion. *Life* magazine got in touch with Theodore S. White, who was then vacationing in Europe. White is an old friend of the Kennedys and *Life* asked him if he would approach Mrs. Kennedy and measure her feelings about serialization. *Look* took a more direct route. It sent Warren Rogers, the chief of its Washington bureau, to speak to Senator Kennedy.

Rogers met the Senator on July 27, two days before the bids on the serialization were to be submitted. Now, it is reasonable to think that *The Death of a President,* no matter how important it was to its author, had not been uppermost on the Senator's mind that summer. In the last month, in alliance with the reform movement, he had beaten the regular Democrats in New York over a nomination for Judge of the Surrogate Court, thereby making it official that he was the most important Democrat in the state. He had also laid the cornerstone for a university in Ethiopia, seen the Pope in a private audience, shot some rapids in Idaho with an astronaut, been cheered at the Calgary Stampede, and marched in a Puerto Rican parade. A poll by the Des Moines *Register* showed that, as a Presidential candidate, he could carry conservative Iowa over George Romney and that Romney could beat Lyndon Johnson. The National Conference for New Politics, a coalition of the New Left, said it was interested in him for President, and Senator Wayne Morse said that he was, too. Meanwhile, the Los Angeles *Times* took a sounding among California Democrats and said that twice as many of them preferred him to Johnson as a candidate.

On the evening that Kennedy met Rogers he was busier than usual. The nation's airlines had been struck and he was part of a Senate committee that was hearing testimony about it. It was not until seven in the evening that he and the *Look* man got together in a room adjacent to the committee room.

As Rogers recalls it, he told Kennedy that *Look* was interested in serializing the manuscript and he asked him if he had read it. Kennedy said no, and that he had no intention of ever reading it. Seigenthaler and Guthman, Kennedy said, were reading it for him "as sort of agents." Either one, he said, but particularly Seigenthaler, could deal with the magazine bids.

Then, according to Rogers, Kennedy said that Manchester had volunteered to turn over his proceeds from the book to the Kennedy Library and that his only real profit would be from the sale of the serialization rights. The Senator, Rogers says, said that Manchester was entitled to get whatever he could from it. Kennedy went on to say that John Kennedy had "thought highly" of Manchester and that he, the Senator, was "favorable" about *Look*'s acquiring the serialization rights.

The conversation has some meaning. Later Dick Goodwin said that when the squabble began it had nothing at all to do with money because the Senator and Mrs. Kennedy thought that the money from the *Look* serialization was going to the library. Therefore, he asked, why would the Kennedys have been upset about money if they thought Manchester was not going to get any of it? But if Rogers' recollection is true, then the Senator, if not Mrs. Kennedy, knew exactly who would get the *Look* money.

Kennedy emphasized to Rogers that he was staying in the background of the negotiations and that Manchester would handle them because it was his book. Seigenthaler, he said, would be the only one exercising any supervision over his interest. Rogers recalls that the talk lasted perhaps ten or fifteen minutes and that at its conclusion, Kennedy punched him lightly on the arm and said: "Call John, and if there is anything I can do, let me know."

The next day Rogers called the editors in New York and told them of the conversation. It was what they had expected.

Look thought that *Life* would be its chief competitor in the bidding, and *Look* had no reason to think that *Life* was one of the Senator's favorite publications. Indeed, Time-Life had never been particularly kind to Democrats, while *Look* was on the best of terms with the Kennedys. Two days before, in fact, *Look* had in hand the first office copies of its issue for August 23. Its cover showed Robert Kennedy in three-quarter profile, bronzed, mouth partly open, apparently absorbed in a debate or a conversation that was calling forth strong emotions. There was nothing recognizable in the background of the cover picture, just dark shadows and light. Inside the issue was a story called "Suppose God Is Black" by Senator Robert F. Kennedy. It told of his trip to South Africa that summer and of how he had debated university students and visited compounds of blacks in the land of apartheid. Negotiations for the story had begun even before the Senator left.

Look had other things going for it, too. It had serialized Ted Sorensen's story of the Kennedy Administration, *Kennedy*, and had left its author and the Kennedy family happy. *Life* had serialized *A Thousand Days,* Schlesinger's story of the Administration, and its treatment of the book and the publicity it got had caused unhappiness among the Kennedys.

The editors were touching all bases, however, and on the same day that Rogers called, Bill Arthur traveled to Middletown to speak to Manchester. He met the author in his office in the library and Manchester told him of his experiences in writing the book. Before he left, Arthur asked Manchester if he would write to him later and list perhaps twenty things in the book that had never before been reported. After *Look* had acquired the serialization rights, Arthur received the letter. It listed nearly forty things.

Arthur did not know it on the afternoon of his visit but early that morning Manchester had called Angie Novello at her home in Washington and asked her again about the elusive telegram. She wrote a memo about it to the Senator:

> Bill Manchester called me at home about the attached letter. I told him I promised to see that you'd work on it today. He said the deadline is 5 P.M. tomorrow.

Another memo dated that same day says:

> I talked to Bill Manchester, who hasn't slept in three nights worrying about that letter. He was assured by John [Seigenthaler] that you'd send it. I explained that you just didn't have time to do it, that you were most anxious to get to it, etc. He said he's meeting with the people from *Life* and *Look* tomorrow, the two he's chosen as the best magazine media for the book, and he would hope that you would rely on his decision on which one should have it and if not should he say the decision is up to you? He'd like to hear from you tonight or from me what you've decided. He hopes to leave with his family on Monday for Maine. (Having reread the above it sounds like Bill was mad and annoyed. He isn't. He's just worried for the book and he wants the best magazine deal because it will make more money for the library.)

Rogers recalls the Senator saying that the money for the magazine serialization would be Manchester's big source of profit. Miss Novello's memorandum to Kennedy indicates that the money from a magazine would go to the Kennedy Library. The fact is that no one was very sure of what the financial arrangements were, and this confusion grew and compounded itself in the next few days.

Shortly after Miss Novello wrote the last memorandum, Kennedy showed up in his office. She told him about Manchester's most recent call and then she began to tell him of the suggestion by Evan Thomas that he send the telegram not to Manchester but to him. Kennedy interrupted her midway. "Send the telegram to Manchester," he said. Miss Novello did, and then she sent a special delivery letter to Thomas that repeated the telegram. The telegram said:

> Should any inquiries arise re the manuscript of your book I would like to state the following:
>
> While I have not read William Manchester's account of the death of President Kennedy, I know of the President's respect for Mr. Manchester as an historian and a reporter. I understand others have plans to publish books regarding the events of November 22, 1963. As this is going to be the subject matter of a book and since Mr. Manchester in his research had access to more information and sources than any other writer, members of the Kennedy family will place no obstacle in the way of publication of his work.
>
> However, if Mr. Manchester's account is published in segments or excerpts, I would expect that incidents would not be taken out of context or summarized in any way which might distort the facts of or the events relating to President Kennedy's death.
>
> ROBERT F. KENNEDY

The telegram, which had originally been drafted by Thomas and then revised slightly by Seigenthaler, was also edited by Kennedy. For one thing, he changed the "assassination of President Kennedy" to the "death of President Kennedy." The original had also said that "I together with other members of our family know of the President's respect for Mr. Manchester as an historian and a reporter." Kennedy deleted the phrase "together with other members of our family." More important, perhaps, the original had said that "I would hope that incidents would not be taken out of context." The Senator had changed "hope" to "expect."

In the affidavit he filed in support of Mrs. Kennedy's suit, the Senator insisted that the telegram was sent at the urging of Manchester and Harper & Row. "I was told by Harper's representatives," he said, "that Manchester was becoming ill from an obsession with the thought that the book might never be published." Kennedy went on to declare that "a careful reading of the language shows that the telegram contains neither a waiver of any of the approval rights of plaintiff [Mrs. Kennedy] or myself nor an approval of the mode or timing of publication or of the text of the manuscript. Both before and after the sending of the telegram, Evan Thomas of Harper & Row and defendant Manchester repeatedly assured me and others associated with me that nothing would be published without the approval of Mrs. Kennedy and myself."

The bids on the serialization were due at 5 P.M. the next day, and there was a feeling in magazine offices that bidding would be high, as well as wild speculation about how high it might be. Evan Thomas, a book and not a magazine man, but still knowledgeable about these things, told the Kennedys that he thought something around $150,000 would win. He was wrong. No one at *Look* had a very clear idea either, and the editors were divided among themselves as to whether *The Death of a President* would fetch a moderately high price, say $150,000, or come in at something extraordinary, perhaps $500,000. *Look* finally decided on a bid of $405,000, which they would offer for the right to serialize the manuscript, the right to sell the serialization to United States and Canadian newspapers after the hardcover book appeared, and the right to sell the serialization to foreign publications. If, however, the newspaper and world rights were sold elsewhere, then *Look* would cut $100,000 from its bid and offer $305,000.

Shortly before 5 P.M. on July 29, Bill Arthur and Bob Meskill, a managing editor, arrived at Congdon's office with the bid. However, this was no ordinary deal, and Arthur, who is tall and slender and comes on as rather a reserved and unemotional man, accompanied the bid with a letter:

JULY 29, 1966

DEAR DON AND BILL:

Enclosed is *Look*'s response to your letter of July 18, 1966, in which you transmitted the manuscript entitled *The Death of a President* by William Manchester.

I have lived with this manuscript for slightly more than one week. But, it seems to me, all of us have lived with it for almost three years. This manuscript is history. It is a part of each of us. It is five days—no more, no less—in the lives of all of us. And yet, it is much more than that. It is us. It is our times. It is our lives, our being, our triumphs, and alas, our tragedy.

Last night, in the Larchmont Avenue Presbyterian Church, a memorial service was held for one of our local boys, a Marine, who died in Viet Nam. Every seat was occupied. There hadn't been such a large crowd since Easter.

As I sat there, I thought about *The Death of a President*. I had just spent about an hour and a half with you, Bill, in Middletown, Conn. I realized, as I talked with you, how you felt about the death of President Kennedy and how deeply the writing of the book affected you. Much of your anguish was shared by those of us who have read your work.

"The Death of a Soldier," I said to myself. This boy, who was memorialized last night, was a soldier. He had volunteered for the Fleet Marines, and for duty in Viet Nam. And he was killed, at the age of 20.

I thought of the lines from Simonides at Thermopylae that you used in the pages preceding your accounting of those four days:

"Go, stranger, and in Lakedaimon tell
That here, obedient to their laws, we fell."

As the Editor of *Look*, I want our magazine to be the vehicle through which we are reminded again, that a young man lived, and, "Obedient to their laws, fell." He, too, was a soldier.

Arthur, of course, was being emotional, which is a pleasant thing to behold, since the conventional wisdom is that magazine editors are spare and driven men full of guile and cold calculation. Nonetheless, Arthur needed something more than warmth and good intentions. *Life* had submitted a bid for $500,000, and Congdon told him so. Earlier, however, Congdon had said that the serialization rights might not go to the magazine with the highest initial bid, and so he decided not to close the bidding. For one thing, Manchester insisted that he have some control over the advertising, layouts, pictures, even the captions that accompanied the serialization. *Life* was reluctant to grant it to him; *Look* was not.

Arthur spoke several times that evening to Gardner Cowles, the head of Cowles Communications, and it was decided to raise *Look*'s bid to $665,000. *Life,* meanwhile, was raising its bid to $600,000. Arthur took the old bid, crossed out the figure of $405,000, and wrote in the new one. His palms, he said, were sweating. *Look* wanted *The Death of a President* badly. So did Arthur.

That evening, just before *Look* made its new offer, Manchester called Kennedy and told him that *Life* was Number One. Kennedy, he says, was apprehensive. "If you pick *Look* you don't have to check with me," the Senator said, "but if it's *Life* I want to talk about it." Senator Kennedy never publicly confirmed that he acquiesced in the magazine sale, but he had. Whether or not he knew that Manchester considered the manuscript completely edited and fully approved is something else. Kennedy says that Manchester told him that night that nothing would be published that did not have the approval of both Mrs. Kennedy and himself. Of course he told him so, Manchester says. Hadn't the manuscript already been approved? Nothing would be published that wasn't in the manuscript. *Ergo,* things were fine, and the finest of all things was that Kennedy's telegram had reached

Manchester. That afternoon he had wired Congdon: "Long awaited RFK telegram of release has arrived and is perfect in every respect."

A few hours later, still euphoric, he wrote another letter to Kennedy.

JULY 29, 1966
8:30 P.M.

DEAR BOB:

It seems a little absurd to be writing you now, since by tomorrow at this time we'll probably have talked about serial rights. My phone has been ringing off and on since noon. College classmates and friends I haven't heard from for years have been phoning me, trying to twist my arm. I feel a little rubbery as a result, but I'm holding the line on control of text *and* layouts, and, in fact, there have been no recent protests about that. I can guarantee you that it will be handled with dignity and taste, and with not the faintest tinge of sensationalism. I can guarantee it because I'm the man who will be making the decisions.

Evan called me to say that he would be seeing you Monday. He'll know my August address—I'll be in Maine, working on serialization cuts. As I indicated on the phone, after things have settled down I'd like to come to Washington and have a talk. I want to be sure you are kept posted on developments, and the author is the best possible source, even better than the editor. In addition, my business is information. Getting it, and getting it straight, has been my preoccupation for almost twenty years.

Your telegram to me was superb. It covered everything and was airtight. I instantly had a Xerox made for Evan. (Last April Liz Moynihan put Pat's income tax return in a machine. It didn't come out. She had to call Pat and say, "Xerox swallowed your 1040." *Then* she had to disassemble the machine. She was late to a party at my house, anyhow, and gave that excuse. I told her it was terrible, that she'd been reading too much Buchwald.)

Thank God for John Seigenthaler and Ed Guthman. Their suggestions, always offered gracefully, were invaluable to the book. It must be extraordinary to be the leader of men like that—more, to know that they are envied because they are so trusted.

There is so much ahead. I pray I'm there to see it, perhaps even to help it along a little.

Now, Manchester had not seen Jackie Kennedy for more than two years. The full horror of the assassination had lain upon her then, and besides enlisting Manchester's boundless sympathies she had won his fidelity. *The Death of a President* joined them inseparably, he thought. It was their bond, the symbol of their joint devotion to John F. Kennedy, and Bill Manchester wanted Jackie Kennedy to know about it and to know that things were right. After he wrote to Bobby Kennedy he wrote to her.

JULY 29, 1966

DEAR JACKIE:

You're too young to remember the abdication of Edward VII [*sic*] (a year younger than Caroline is now, think of it), but it was the greatest story since the Resurrection, and I can still remember his opening words: "At long last I am able to say a few words of my own. I have never wanted to withhold anything, but until now it was not constitutionally possible for me to speak."

Until now it has not been *procedurally* possible for me to speak. Four months ago we agreed to set up an elaborate system of readers of my manuscript, and to remove the personal element an elaborate chain of command was set up. I dealt with Evan Thomas. Evan talked to the readers. The readers talked to Bob. Now and then we would all get together on coast-to-coast conference calls (which I detest, because you never know to whom you're speaking), but most of us knew only the men above and below. Like spies.

But today Bob's long telegram approving the revised manuscript for January 25 publication, preceded by the usual fanfare, ends the chain. And so, at long last, I am able to say a few words of my own.

Not being a king, and not having a *soignée* divorcee by my side, I feel tongue-tied. The publishing world is talking of the book in the most extravagant terms—I have a little modesty left, so I shan't set them down here—but my only thought is to get away from it and dive into something else. How can I possibly feel pride in a manuscript based upon the greatest national tragedy of this century? I can't. If they give me a great big prize rolled in gold and polished to blind the cosmos, I'll just say "Thanks."

Everyone who has read it agrees that you shouldn't, not ever. Don't be tempted by curiosity or the suggestions of stupid people. It will just bring back all the sadness.

Yet I do want you to know that nothing was spared to make certain that the book was as good as it could be. Five gifted Kennedy men—John Seigenthaler, Ed Guthman, Arthur Schlesinger, Dick Goodwin, and Evan Thomas—read every line, and some read it three times. Their suggestions have been incorporated in the manuscript, and they are good suggestions. For example, though I tried desperately to suppress my bias against a certain eminent statesman who always reminds me of somebody in a Grade D movie on the late show, the prejudice showed through. That was cheap of me, but I suppose there is a little meanness in all of us. This man had lied to me twice, among other things; he is not what my father called...a gentleman.... So that, among other things, was cut. The result is a stronger, more dispassionate book. Harper's is so certain that it will be read 100 years from now that after the title, *The Death of a President*, there will be the subtitle *November 20–November 25, 1963.* Otherwise, they feel, future generations might confuse it with books about Lincoln.

The safeguards have not ended. I have tied the tightest strings in publishing history to serial use of the text. Indeed, two editors, both men I respect, refused to read it unless I gave them a free hand. I shan't do that. I insist that I approve, not only the condensation, but layouts, pictures, heads, and that I play a role in any promotional material.

I've even suggested the book jacket. Harper's likes it. It's very simple. Just the sky at night. *Not* black, but a deep blue heaven, studded with clouds of stars, and the lettering, a dignified white-on-red with broad, stately serifs.

Perhaps I've only persuaded myself that the President would be proud of the scholarship and the style. But all of the readers so far have agreed with me. At any rate, I gave it my best, which, of course, was little enough.

It would be nice to talk to you some relaxed afternoon; I'll be in Maine during August, working on the serial cuts— Evan Thomas will know how to reach me—and I'll be back on campus the first week in September.

The next day, Saturday, July 30, only *Look* and *Life* were still in the competition. *The Saturday Evening Post,* which had been the only other magazine that had submitted a bid anywhere near that of *Look* and *Life,* had dropped out overnight. Bill Arthur decided to spend Saturday on the tennis court at the Orienta Yacht Club in Mamaroneck, New York. The yacht club is on Long Island Sound, and Arthur, if his vision was good enough, might have looked over the water and seen the managing editor of *Life,* George P. Hunt, who chose that day to work on his boat. Arthur had an inestimable advantage over Hunt. He was near a phone; Hunt was not. Arthur made and received a good many calls that day. Among others, he spoke to Gardner Cowles, Don Congdon, and John Seigenthaler, and the most important one was Seigenthaler, who told him that Hunt was on his boat and that the other *Life* editors had dispersed for the weekend. He suggested to Arthur that he call Congdon and demand that a 5 P.M. deadline be observed for the receipt of bids. Seigenthaler knew that Hunt did not plan to leave the boat until 6 P.M. Consequently, Arthur did call Congdon and insist on a deadline. At five fifteen Congdon called him. He said that *Look* had won—at $665,000.

A jubilant Manchester phoned Kennedy a few minutes later. The Senator was at Hyannisport and he left the tennis court there to come to the phone. As Manchester recalls the conversation, he told Kennedy of the price and the Senator said: "Great; isn't that a record? *Look* has been so nice to the family and Henry Luce has been such a bastard."

Kennedy was right about the price; it was a record for serialization rights. A few days later Mike Land, the senior editor at *Look* who had read the manuscript first, called another senior editor from Texas. Land was on vacation and he and his wife had stopped off to see Bob Oswald, the brother of Lee Harvey Oswald, who was also preparing a book with the help of Land and his wife. "Gary," Land asked, "how did the bidding go?" *Look* had bid $665,000, Gereon Zimmermann told him. Land thought that Zimmermann was confused, that he meant a bid in six figures. No, Zimmermann assured him, it was $665,000. Land was surprised. He had never thought that it would be that high. He was not alone in this. Jackie Kennedy had never thought it would be that high either.

Five

─────── ∿ ───────

JACQUELINE KENNEDY had spent June of 1966 in the Hawaiian Islands with her children. She had leased a beach house from Senator Peter Dominick of Colorado, visited Laurance Rockefeller's ranch house on the island of Hawaii and picnicked at an isolated beach on Kauai, which she had reached by helicopter. "I had forgotten and my children had never known," she said, "what it is like to discover a new place, unwatched and unnoticed." When she left the islands she thanked the newspapers in Honolulu for their "extraordinary gesture" of not bothering her. Then Mrs. Kennedy returned to New York and from there she was driven to Newport, Rhode Island, where she attended the wedding of her half-sister, Janet Jennings Auchincloss. Tourists mobbed the wedding, of course.

Mrs. Kennedy returned to Hyannisport in time to celebrate her thirty-seventh birthday on July 28 at a party given by Mr. and Mrs. Paul Mellon. Mellon is a financier and art collector, and the guests were all pretty much celebrated, too. There was Secretary of Defense Robert S. McNamara and his wife; Mike Nichols, the actor and director; Samuel Barber, the composer; the Leonard Bernsteins; Ambassador David Bruce and his wife, who flew from England for the party; Billy Baldwin, a decorator; Oliver Smith, the Broadway set designer; Mr. and Mrs. Frederick Cushing; the Jock Whitneys, who arrived by yacht; the Averell Harrimans; Mr. and Mrs. William Paley of the Columbia Broadcasting System, and even Mr. Kenneth, Mrs. Kennedy's hairdresser.

In none of her activities was Mrs. Kennedy involved with either *The Death of a President* or the machinations that were surrounding it. She did not enter the picture at all until July 31, 1966, when Robert Kennedy told her of the sale and of the amount that *Look* had paid. Richard Goodwin, the former adviser to her husband who later acted as her spokesman, insists that Mrs. Kennedy was never disturbed by the amount of money. Jackie Kennedy, he says, became disturbed about *The Death of a President* only when she heard that Manchester was speaking about an "approved manuscript." This, however, is only part of it. On August 1, the day after Mrs. Kennedy heard about the sale, Thomas told Manchester that she was upset about the large sum involved. Thomas had spoken to Robert Kennedy, who apparently had said something about the library not getting enough money. Manchester was in genuine confusion. He tried to call the Senator at Hyannisport and reached instead Ethel Kennedy, Bobby's wife. Of all the Kennedy family, Manchester retains probably the kindest memories of Ethel. He doesn't know why this is so, but it may be because he thinks she is without guile. "Ethel," he says, "is a sweet girl."

Manchester had decided that he would tell Senator Kennedy that others who had written about the President—Schlesinger, Salinger, and Sorensen, for instance—had done their research while they were members of the Administration and that he had done his research alone, without official protection, indeed, without getting paid other than an advance. Furthermore, he would point out that he would be the largest single contributor to the Kennedy Library, giving more, say, than Standard Oil or General Motors. He didn't get to say any of these things, however, because he couldn't reach the Senator. (In fact, he never got to say these things to the Senator, not then, or in the next few months.) Manchester asked Ethel Kennedy how Jackie was, and if she was really disturbed about the money that *Look* was giving him. Ethel said no, don't worry because she and Jean Kennedy Smith had spoken to Jackie and Jackie now had a better idea of what the *Look* serialization was all about. Thanks, said Manchester, but he would call Bob in Washington anyway.

Whereupon Manchester called Kennedy in Washington, and reached instead Angie Novello, his private secretary. She said the Senator was in a committee meeting, but that she would pass him a note and call him back. She did, and she said that the Senator had passed the note back with another note that said, Manchester recalls, "Tell him I always keep my word and I mean to in this case." Somewhat reassured, but not very much, Manchester wrote another letter to Kennedy. This one said that in the future it would be better if they spoke to one another directly rather than through intermediaries.

Kennedy did not answer, and Thomas, trying to mediate, or at least to say something that might soothe somebody, wrote to Angie Novello. He did not know if he should write to the Senator directly, he said, and so he thought he would write to her, and when she thought the time was ripe she could pass it on to him.

He wrote:

> I am sure we can work it out so that the *Look* money goes directly to the library and I can assure you that this company will cut its profits to take nothing more than a fair percentage of return of net trade volume, a return to be guided

by the past fiscal year's experience (of 6 per cent after taxes)
and this will make it possible I think for us to make the
loss to the author occasioned by special gifting over and
above that spelled out in the original agreement between
Manchester, Harper, and RFK. (Cutting largely into even
the publisher's reduced share of book club reprinting.) I will
be happy to make a specific proposal and to invite an ac-
countant nominated by Bobby Kennedy to discuss it with
me should he wish.

Thomas was acting on the theory that all would be well
if the money was not a problem. It might have been, too,
but then Homer Bigart complicated things. Homer Bigart
is a stocky, middle-aged man with a flushed face and a stam-
mer. He is also a genius, who has won two Pulitzer Prizes
and a potful of lesser honors for writing stories from nearly
everywhere in the world. *The New York Times* had told
Homer to find out something about the Manchester book
and he had found out that *Look* had just promised to pay
a fabulous sum for the right to serialize it. Homer called
Manchester, whom he had run across in Karachi years before,
he called Evan Thomas, and he called people at *Look*. Everyone was evasive, or at least sufficiently evasive so that he
couldn't find out quite everything. Bigart, however, had succeeded in making Thomas nervous. The editor feared that
he might read about all that had been happening in the
paper the next morning, and so he and Manchester wired
Kennedy:

> Homer Bigart of *Times* is on to book and serial story and
> has gathered many facts including price of sale. We have
> been evasive in our replies regarding money. Under existing
> terms we expect book to be largest single contributor to
> library and are delighted with that prospect. In the absence
> of any further discussion we must assume that original signed
> agreement prevails.

On the face of it, it is a perfectly straightforward telegram, incapable of misinterpretation. In his affidavit, Senator Kennedy said he found it perfectly clear and that he answered it with another perfectly clear telegram that said:

> Re telegram where you say quote in absence of any instructions signed agreement prevails unquote. Agree, and that provides that Mrs. Kennedy and I must give permission for publication of book and that has not yet been given.

A careful reader will note that the Senator has misquoted the telegram from Thomas and Manchester slightly, but this is of no great importance. According to Senator Kennedy's affidavit, the telegram from Manchester and Thomas was proof positive that both knew the manuscript had not been approved. After all, he said, they wrote that the "signed agreement prevails." What else could they be referring to but the original memorandum of understanding? As in all things connected with *The Death of a President,* however, the truth is slightly obscure.

Thomas insists that the "signed agreement" in his telegram referred to the contract between Manchester and Harper & Row, specifically the section that dealt with Manchester's royalties. Furthermore, he says, the Senator knew this. Thomas says that when he sent it he was only trying to get Kennedy to answer his earlier proposal for a new financial arrangement that would give the Kennedy Library a bigger share of money from the *Look* sale.

Nonetheless, when Kennedy read the telegram he was annoyed, and he said that he considered it a form of "blackmail." Apparently, he was having second thoughts about the telegram he sent on July 28 in which he said that "members of the Kennedy family will place no obstacle in the way of publication" of *The Death of a President,* and he feared that Thomas and Manchester were trying to tell him that approval of the manuscript was an accomplished fact. He spoke to Thomas on the phone and told him that he considered the telegram from him and Manchester to be an "angry" one. Thomas said he did not intend it that way and that he was only expressing his concern about the financial arrangements. According to Thomas, Kennedy told him this was fine, and that he was pleased to have everything cleared up. Later, Thomas says, he received the telegram that the Senator quoted in his affidavit, only it was not from the Senator at all. It was from Angie Novello, and it said:

> Bob dictated following before conversation with you today: Re telegram where you say quote in absence of any instructions signed agreement prevails unquote. Agree, and that provides that Mrs. Kennedy and I must give permission for publication of the book and that has not yet been given.

It was signed: Angie.

After the telegram arrived, Thomas called Manchester, who had begun a vacation in Maine, and told him that Kennedy had misunderstood their telegram and that he and Jackie weren't concerned about the manuscript; it was the money, he said.

That same day, Manchester, still perplexed, called Arthur Schlesinger, who was getting ready to leave for a weekend in Hyannisport. Manchester said he had not heard from Kennedy directly and he asked Schlesinger to intervene if he could and to find out what was bothering whom. Two days later, Manchester recalls, Schlesinger returned the call and said that he had spoken to both the Senator and Mrs. Kennedy the night before. Both, he said, were calm, although Jackie was a little "jittery" about the prospect of serialization.

Either Manchester's recollection of what Schlesinger said is faulty or else the historian was trying to soothe Manchester.

The Kennedys were upset. At least part of the problem was that Robert Kennedy and William Manchester did not really exist in the same world. The Senator was a politician, and Manchester was a writer. Robert Kennedy does not customarily deal with people he considers eccentric, and when he does he is not very good at it, and he would prefer that the world not know about it. Both Seigenthaler and Guthman had told Warren Rogers of *Look* that they were not having special problems editing the manuscript when in fact they were. Neither Guthman nor Seigenthaler, however, wanted to draw attention to them.

Part of the stigmata of being a Kennedy is that virtually anything that happens to you is news, and sometimes it is big news. We, all of us, are locked in a gigantic embrace with the Kennedys. We have made them charismatic when perhaps they were not, and we have asked—even demanded—that we be admitted into their lives. When Caroline goes to college she will be photographed by men from the wire services, every paper and television station in the country will carry the pictures, and a whole generation of Americans will sit and sigh and recall that day in Dallas, and know that it is growing older, and where has the time gone?

Perhaps this is the way it should be. The Kennedys are a fact of our existence, like urbanization, the Gross National Product, and underdeveloped countries. When John Kennedy was elected President in 1960 the United States began a new era in politics. Henceforth, political style would be measured against his, and style is not a small thing in mid-twentieth-century America. When John Kennedy died, millions of young people fell from innocence, knowing for the first time the monstrous irrationalities that can change their lives. Subsequently, Robert Kennedy and Edward Kennedy became figures in the land, and even the least critical of their supporters knew that, in the beginning at least, the most

important things they had going for them was the name
Kennedy. Ted Kennedy was thirty years old and an assistant
district attorney in Boston when he announced for the Senate. Robert Kennedy joined him there later after campaign-
ing and winning in a state in which he did not live.

A mystique envelops the Kennedys; there are few political
observers who do not think that Robert Kennedy will be a
candidate for President by 1972. There are few who would
rule out Ted Kennedy for some time after that. These things
are not improbable, but they are delicate and they require
very special handling. After all, there is an assumption about
the Kennedys: they are arrogant. There is truth to this, of
course, although the political Kennedys usually carry arrogance with grace and flare. Without it they might be just
uppity Boston Irish with money. Still, arrogance has its limi-
tations, and in itself it does not win elections. Robert Kennedy knows this and he knows there is this picture of the
arrogant, ruthless Bobby Kennedy, without grace and flare,
who crushes everyone who gets in his way. He is not a notably
impetuous man and he would rather not be thought of as
arrogant. It may be assumed that he thought it over rather
carefully before August 10, 1966, when he decided to try to
prevent the publication of *The Death of a President*. On
that day he sent a telegraphed day letter to Evan Thomas.
It said:

> Under the present circumstances, with the situation as
> difficult as it is, I feel the book on President Kennedy's death
> should neither be published nor serialized. I would appre-
> ciate it if you would inform Bill Manchester.
> As you know only too well, this has been a trying situa-
> tion for everyone and I understand the problems this situa-
> tion has caused you and the author.
> It just seems to me that rather than struggling with this
> any longer we should take our chances with Jim Bishop.

Coming as it did, less than two weeks after Robert Kennedy had said that the Kennedy family would place no obstacle in the way of publication, the day letter is a remarkable piece of correspondence. Manchester had devoted two years of his life to preparing the book, and nearly everyone who read it had agreed that, despite some lapses in taste and judgment, it was an extraordinary piece of work. *Look* magazine was prepared to pay $665,000 to serialize it, and Harper & Row had already sent a piece of it to the printers. Although Kennedy only said that "I feel" the book should not be published, the intent of the message was clear: stop the book.

Robert Kennedy was taking a risk when he sent the message. He was opening himself to a nasty charge of book burning, and he was being unkind to the family chronicler, which would not make him look like a nice guy. Robert Kennedy is not obtuse. He must have known all these things, and he does not do things without cause. He sent the message because Jackie Kennedy was raising hell.

Mrs. Kennedy had not had much to do with the book before August. When Manchester wrote to her the night before the serialization rights were sold to *Look* and spoke about an "approved manuscript," the letter was answered by Pamela Turnure, Mrs. Kennedy's secretary, who simply noted that it had been received. Miss Turnure had read the book and prepared a long memorandum about it. She asked for seventy-seven changes, and she sent both Mrs. Kennedy and Manchester a copy of the memorandum. Some of the changes she sought were factual corrections: the woman who gave President Kennedy French lessons was not Mademoiselle Hirsch, but Madame Hirsch. Others were less obvious: changing "healing the unhealable" to "repairing the unrepairable," deleting a passage about Cardinal Cushing's medical history. Mostly, however, Pamela wanted great swatches of copy taken out that dealt with Jackie Kennedy, and she took a far more severe view of what ought to be taken out than had Seigenthaler, Guthman, or Thomas.

It would be a mistake, however, to think that Miss Turnure was acting alone, that it was she, not Mrs. Kennedy, who was demanding the changes. In her suit to suppress the book, Mrs. Kennedy declared that she had never read *The Death of a President,* and she said that she "cannot be said to have approved what I have never seen." Nonetheless, the memo by Miss Turnure is full of citations marked "delete" or "Ibid.," without any description of the material involved and without explanation of why it ought to be deleted. Presumably, they were explained to Mrs. Kennedy.

It has never been quite clear when Mrs. Kennedy read the manuscript. Her partisans say she never read it at all. Yet she read at least a large part of the material that *Look* wanted to serialize in a meeting one Saturday morning in an attorney's office on Wall Street. She emerged from the meeting in tears, but not because of the manuscript. She was annoyed because there were two reporters outside and she had thought that the meeting was a secret. Manchester also claims to have positive knowledge that she read the manuscript at least once —when the suit was within hours of reaching the court. This, he says, is what led to the settlement.

Mrs. Kennedy had not liked *White House Nannie,* Maude Shaw's book, and she had not liked *The Pleasure of His Company,* Paul Fay's book. Both were slender, unpresumptuous works, but at her request, passages were excised in both. *The Death of a President* was something else. It was neither slender nor unpretentious, and it promised to be a best seller. Mrs. Kennedy found much to object to. There were passages that told of her thoughts and actions as she stood by her husband's coffin. There were copies of letters that she and her daughter had written to the President, a description of how she slipped her wedding ring on his finger in Parkland Hospital. There was an account of how Maude Shaw, not Mrs. Kennedy, had told Caroline of her father's death. (Manchester was adamant about retaining this section. "But it cannot go," he wrote to a friend. "I will take anything but that.") There was a description of Mrs. Kennedy as she sat at her dressing table, searching her face for wrinkles, a painful account of how she had spent the night of her husband's death alone in bed at the White House, writhing and tossing while under sedation. There were at least twenty-five areas in the book to which she had truly strong objections, and many of the objections could not be met by changing a word here and a word there. They demanded major revisions. Even more, they demanded that the author find a new orientation, a new approach to his work. He had written a highly personal account, an emotional retelling of the assassination.

Evan Thomas and Arthur Schlesinger had considered Manchester's portrait of John Kennedy too romantic, making him too much the young prince and not enough of the world leader. Manchester may have done that, but he did something else, too. He drew John Kennedy as a man with some earthy caprices. There was a scene in the book in which John Kennedy distractedly padded around a bedroom in his shorts and mused about politics. His secretary, a woman of some sophistication, entered the room and hoped that he would put his pants on before anyone else saw him. Mrs. Kennedy objected to this representation of her husband, presumably because it made him look undignified, which it did. However, it also made John Kennedy a more endearing figure, and it was probably as accurate a picture of him as either Manchester's young prince or Schlesinger's world leader.

Mrs. Kennedy also objected to the use of a letter she had written to her husband from Greece. The letter was deleted from the book, but it did appear in *Stern,* the magazine that bought the German serialization rights from *Look* and then refused to abide by the agreement that *Look* reached with Mrs. Kennedy on revising the serialization. The letter, which was reprinted in American newspapers, was charming; it made Jacqueline Kennedy look like a warm and good wife. Manchester apparently thought so, too, but Mrs. Kennedy had strong objections to its use. Clearly, there was a great gap between the author and Mrs. Kennedy on what the book was all about.

When Robert Kennedy's day letter on canceling publication reached Evan Thomas there was consternation. Manchester was scheduled to sign the contract with *Look* magazine the next day and an important section of the contract said that Robert Kennedy, speaking for other members of the Kennedy family, had approved publication of the manuscript. It was altogether fitting that Manchester had chosen *Look* to serialize his book; it kept things in the family.

While Harper & Row would not profit at all from the sale of the rights, the publishing company had some loose connections with Cowles Communications, which puts out *Look*. John Cowles, Jr., a nephew of Gardner Cowles, the chairman of Cowles, is the editor of the Minneapolis *Star and Tribune,* which owns half of *Harper's* magazine. The other half is owned by Harper & Row. John Cowles, Jr., is the president of Harper's and serves on its board with Cass Canfield, the head of Harper & Row. Furthermore, Canfield is his father-in-law. John Cowles married the former Sage Fuller, a daughter of Mr. Canfield's second wife.

Family connections notwithstanding, the editors at *Look* were more excited about the manuscript than their counterparts at Harper & Row. The excitement touched not only the editors; it got to their secretaries, too. Mike Land had prepared an extract of 100,000 words on which *Look* would base its serialization. The secretaries vied with one another for the privilege of typing it so they could read it.

Bill Arthur, the editor who had written to Manchester and his agent and drawn the parallel between President Kennedy and the young soldier who had been killed in Vietnam, says that "from the very beginning our whole idea was to do this with dignity and to avoid sensationalism. There was never any thought about using pictures of the assassination or of doing anything that would detract from the dignity of the story." Consequently, when *Look* heard about Robert Kennedy's decision to cancel publication it was disturbed, but not shattered. It put off the signing of the contract from August 11 to August 12, which was the same day that Manchester met with the Senator at his office in Washington.

The meeting had been arranged through the good offices of Harper & Row, but it was not a success. A few days later, when both Manchester and Kennedy were past the point of reasonable argument together, Cass Canfield wrote Mrs. Kennedy that Harper & Row had arranged "for the author to travel to Washington last Friday so that Manchester could tell RFK that he was prepared to divest himself of unusual earnings in any manner that seemed appropriate to the circumstances. Neither the publisher nor the author is seeking a bonanza."

That was the plan and it was doomed from the start. For one thing, Kennedy was presented with the *Look* contract as a *fait accompli*. For another, there is at least a possibility that he and Jackie Kennedy were bothered as much by the fact that *Look* was paying $665,000 for the manuscript as by the fact that Manchester was getting it. There is something about the figure $665,000 that gives pause. It is not uncommon for a magazine to pay $100,000 or even $200,000 for the right to serialize a book, and everyone knows that Hollywood is long accustomed to parting with indecent sums for the privilege of making a movie from a book. Still, it is news when *Look,* which has never been as sensational or as abrasive as *Life,* will spend such a large sum for a book. You do not pay that much for a serious work of history. What was *Look* up to?

Actually, *Look* was up to nothing indecent. It just wanted the book. The Kennedys, however, like most wealthy people, are distrustful when large sums of money are mentioned. The huge sale price could only complicate matters.

Nonetheless, Harper & Row, which still saw itself as not just a publisher but a family friend, too, was acting on the theory that if Manchester would make less money from *Look* all would be well. Harper & Row was even prepared to draw up a new contract with Manchester that would give him more money on the hardcover book. It sounds something like robbing Peter to pay Paul, and it was.

So, on the afternoon of August 12 Evan Thomas and Manchester flew to Washington to meet with Bobby Kennedy and John Seigenthaler. The nation was deep in the airline strike and Thomas and Manchester chartered a single-engine plane for the flight from New York. Everything was arranged. Manchester was to magnanimously divest himself of part of the big *Look* profit, Harper & Row would make it up to him, and the Kennedys would be pleased. Thomas literally rehearsed Manchester in what he would say to the Senator. ("Bob, I never wanted to make a lot of money from this. I'm deeply distressed. Let's see if we can work this out.") In the tiny cabin of the plane, shouting above the roar of the engine, Manchester and Thomas discussed it. The Harper & Row editor was hopeful, if not confident. Surely everyone would be reasonable. Manchester would be conciliatory, and Bobby would do anything to extricate himself from the damned thing.

When they reached the Senator's office, however, the author blew his opening lines. "Well, Bob," he said, "I guess we should be facing each other with dueling pistols and swords." In retrospect, it was not a bad idea. None of the participants at the meeting has a very clear idea of who said what to whom, but all agree that tempers rose and that the conference was a flop.

Thomas sat on one couch, Seigenthaler on another. Manchester sat between them on a chair, and Kennedy stood in his shirtsleeves, pacing back and forth at one end of the room.

"Why can't we stop this *Look* thing?" he asked.

"I have a contract with them," the author said.

"You have a contract with me, too."

"I told you I don't want to get rich out of it and Harper doesn't want to get rich out of it. But I'll tell you one thing. I want to be the man who says how much I'm going to give to the library, and nobody should tell me how much."

Manchester went on to say he had been through a "great deal," that he was under a doctor's care, and that Bobby's telegram on canceling publication had caused him new pain.

"And I am not the only one who has suffered," he said. "I met last night with the editors of *Look* and Evan Thomas in a hotel room, and one of them is sick now and in the care of a doctor." ("Shit," Seigenthaler said later. "He just meant that he had too much to drink.")

"I'm fully aware that you weren't looking for this assignment," Kennedy said. "I know you have been through a great deal. Mrs. Kennedy has been through a great deal, too. And so have I. I just want to review the facts to see if we have an understanding of what the facts are.

"First, you agreed that nothing would appear in *Look* unless Ed [Guthman] and John [Seigenthaler] approved. Second, Evan Thomas assured me that Harper & Row would publish nothing unless there was approval."

"You are quite right, Senator," Thomas interrupted. "We didn't want to publish this book in the first place."

"You and I and Evan talked about this at the outset," Kennedy went on, "and agreed that no one wanted to make the death of President Kennedy a commercial project. And now I just want to know if you are going to live up to this."

At approximately that moment, the argument lost its last hope of a settlement. Voices were raised; Kennedy quickened his pacing; Manchester said again that he had suffered "a great deal." Then he said that *Look* would not allow him to make more changes in the manuscript, and that tore it completely. The last vestige of hope depended on Manchester's being able to revise the manuscript, and now that seemed to be gone.

"Now listen," Seigenthaler said, "I had an understanding with Evan and you that this was not going to be published on the anniversary of the President's death. But with seven installments you'd have the assassination on the stands on the day of the death. [*Look* wanted to publish from October 18, 1966, to January 24, 1967.] This was exactly what you, Evan, said we would be covered against, and what you said would not be done."

"I can't believe it. I just can't believe it," Kennedy said.

"I'll publish the book anytime you want to publish it— or, if you don't want to publish, Senator, that suits me fine. But here's the problem you've got with *Look*. He's signed away his rights."

"They publish on alternate weeks and they would not have an issue on the stands on the anniversary," Manchester explained.

"They'll change their publication date just so that an issue will be out on November twenty-second," said Seigenthaler.

Manchester rose to his feet then and said dramatically:

"Give me the name of the individual to whom I can send my contribution to the library."

Kennedy told him Stephen Smith, his brother-in-law, and Manchester wrote it down. Then Miss Novello entered the room and told the Senator that it was time for him to leave. He had an appointment, and the *Caroline,* the family jet, was waiting at the airport. Kennedy started to go, but Thomas stopped him.

"Look, Bob, this man has put a good deal of himself into this book. He feels very strongly about it. Please don't walk out now. I think you should give him an opportunity to have his say."

"I thought he was through. OK, let's go ahead."

Manchester repeated what he had said before, and said that he would be the "most substantial contributor" of all to the Kennedy Library. Kennedy was not placated.

"You're telling me you're going to put those magazines on the stand. You're going to hurt Mrs. Kennedy in this way. You've refused to stand by a commitment not to get rich, or you said you wouldn't, and now it doesn't mean anything to you. You're going to put Mrs. Kennedy to great pain, great torture—and all the Kennedys. And I can't—I don't believe *Look* will do this."

Then Kennedy asked if Manchester would get the proofs of the *Look* galleys to Seigenthaler and Guthman. Manchester said he could, but that they must be returned in five days. Seigenthaler said dryly that it hardly looked as if Manchester had "tied the tightest string in publishing history" to his book. Kennedy, in turn, demanded that Manchester "shred" the manuscript so that it would be unprintable.

"I can't," Manchester said. *"Look* won't go along. I've got a contract with them."

"You've got a contract with me. You must tell them that. Or tell me who the man up there is and I'll tell him myself. Give me his name. I'll call him now."

Manchester said it was John F. Harding, the vice-president and general counsel for *Look,* and Kennedy left the room. Manchester denies it, but he is supposed to have said then: "There's something wrong. This is not the brother of the man I knew. There's something definitely wrong here."

Kennedy returned and said he had told Harding that he and Mrs. Kennedy were disturbed and that he had asked him to put off publication. Harding told him that *Look* had a contract with Manchester and that it thought the contract was fair and honorable. Nevertheless, he said, he would discuss things with Gardner Cowles.

The meeting broke up then with strained and painful little mutterings. Manchester, however, seemed conciliatory. Kennedy took Thomas aside and told him not to worry about the *Look* serialization and to go ahead and publish the book. Kennedy believed then that Harper & Row would make all the changes he requested; the Senator's position was not so inconsistent as it sounds.

Seigenthaler went to the airport with Manchester and Thomas and there, by the side of the chartered plane, shouting above the engine roar, they spoke once more. Seigenthaler recalls it as a singular conversation. He says he told Manchester that he "had to give a little," and that a solution might lie in making the revisions in the manuscript and persuading *Look* to stay off the newsstands until after the anniversary of the assassination.

But Manchester, Seigenthaler says, insisted there was nothing he could do. Seigenthaler reminded him that he had told Kennedy he would try to cooperate. Now, he said, you're retreating. Seigenthaler says Manchester had explained: "I told Bobby what he wanted to hear."

Manchester stayed that night in the hotel at La Guardia Airport. He had told Harding of the meeting, and Harding asked him to draw up an account of all that had happened since he had first heard from Pierre Salinger more than two years before, and of how, exactly, Robert Kennedy, on behalf of other members of the family, had given him permission to publish his manuscript. Manchester borrowed a typewriter from the office of the hotel manager and sat up most of the night typing it.

In the contract that Manchester and Cowles Communications had signed, the author had given this guarantee:

> That said manuscript was prepared by him with the authorization, consent and cooperation of Mrs. Jacqueline B. Kennedy and Senator Robert F. Kennedy and that Senator Kennedy has, speaking for the Kennedy family, approved the publication of same.

The contract called for the serialization to begin in the *Look* issue of October 18 and to continue through seven installments with the final one in the issue of January 24. Manchester's agent had received $365,000 when the agreement was executed, and it was arranged to pay the final $300,000 in five approximately equal installments, with the first on January 10, 1967, and the final one on January 10, 1971. For this, *Look* had acquired the right to use up to 80,000 words of the manuscript, and it agreed that it would submit first proofs and final photo copies of the article to the author for his approval "so there can be no question [of having] substantially changed the meaning of any of the material."

Look decided that it had a strong case and that it would go ahead with serialization. The decision pleased Manchester, and the day after he delivered his typed recollections to Harding, he was visited by Mike Land, who was as enthusiastic as ever about the manuscript. Land had worked all that day and had reached Middletown by bus in the evening. He was tired, it was raining, and he really just wanted to go to bed. Manchester picked him up at the bus depot and the two men had a leisurely dinner at a restaurant. Then Manchester drove him to his home and said there were just a few things he wanted to discuss about the serialization. They worked until 3 A.M.

Six

IN time, there was a good deal of speculation about Robert Kennedy's shadow cabinet: the men who were advising him and working on *The Death of a President,* and who, presumably, would all be swept into important jobs when he won the Presidency. The prospect of this, it was explained, lay behind their slavish devotion to the Senator and the zeal with which they tried to make right what an author had put asunder.

John Seigenthaler and Ed Guthman, who had been with the Senator when he was Attorney General, could become, respectively, special adviser to the President and White House press secretary. Dick Goodwin, whose Washington apprenticeship had included a turn as Deputy Assistant Secretary of State for Inter-American Affairs, was a cinch for Secretary of State. Pierre Salinger, who, when asked his opinion of Manchester by a reporter, said, "He is purely and simply a welsher who welshed on his contract," would be returned to the White House, too, while Theodore C. Sorensen, who wrote a statement for Mrs. Kennedy in which she excoriated both Manchester and his book, would be pushed by Bobby as the next Senator from New York. Arthur Schlesinger, of course, would be resident intellectual in the new Administration, if John Kenneth Galbraith did not get there first.

Senator Kennedy is surrounded by an extraordinarily talented entourage, all of whom know that he is odds-on to be a President of the United States. The members of the entourage feel a genuine identity of interest with the Senator. Having it, in fact, is a precondition for admission to the entourage, which is a large one. Kennedy's official staff alone is made up of ninety persons, the largest of any Senator. His unofficial staff is far larger. It includes greater and lesser names, and one of the greatest is Burke Marshall, who talks and looks like a grocery clerk from Peoria, and who, for three years as an Assistant Attorney General in charge of the Civil Rights Division, was a scourge of southern sheriffs, southern school boards, and southern registrars. (He, of course, would be Attorney General in the next Administration.)

Marshall, who had left the Government and was a vice-president and general counsel for International Business Machines, made his first appearance in the controversy at a meeting in the Berkshire Hotel in New York on August 15, three days after Manchester had met with Kennedy in Washington. A couple of other new faces showed up, too. They were William Attwood, the new editor-in-chief of Cowles Communications, and Simon H. Rifkind, a former Federal judge, who was now Mrs. Kennedy's attorney. The meeting at the Berkshire marked the decline of Manchester as a really important personality in the battle. He had written the book, and a lot of important people were talking about him, of course, but aside from a few stray meetings he was now on the periphery. Bigger guns had taken over.

On the day of the meeting, for example, there was a

cryptic memo typed and placed in the Senator's files in Washington, and it indicated that the Kennedys wanted to hold Manchester at arm's length. It said:

> P. T. [presumably Pamela Turnure] talked with Jackie and then with Evan Thomas. Passed the message that it would be unwise for her to send anything in writing to Manchester. However, Evan was to tell Manchester emphatically that she had agreed to be interviewed by him only on the basis that she should have the right to destroy the entire transcript ... or decide what should be edited out. Manchester knew this will be breaking his agreement with her, if he does not agree to the changes she wants.

Bill Attwood, as was fitting, had known and liked John F. Kennedy. Now, as a top executive of Cowles, he would argue with his widow and his brother. John Kennedy had asked Attwood to write speeches during the 1960 campaign, and after he won the Presidency, Kennedy had appointed him Ambassador to Kenya and then Ambassador to Guinea. When diplomatic life palled, Attwood had answered a summons from Gardner Cowles to return to an executive suite in the Look Building, where one of the first things he did was to hang a picture of John Kennedy.

It is a fact that a good many people who got involved in the fight on both sides had inscribed pictures of President Kennedy in their homes and offices. Manchester's was in color and it showed Kennedy with the White House in the background. The inscription read: "To Bill Manchester, with warmest regards during his period of portraiture." Side by side on Manchester's bookshelves there were also Schlesinger's *A Thousand Days* and Sorensen's *Kennedy*. *A Thousand Days* is inscribed "with warm regards." On the flyleaf of "Kennedy" it says: "To Bill Manchester, who really cares."

Simon Rifkind, Mrs. Kennedy's attorney, may not have

had the same emotional tie to President Kennedy, but he
at least had been acquainted with him. Kennedy had appointed him to head a fifteen-member commission that considered the controversy over work rules in the railroad
industry. Rifkind did the job with some distinction. Simon
Rifkind is a small man, only five feet six inches tall, and if
he were caricatured he would resemble a rather timid chip-
munk, which would give an absolutely mistaken impression.
Simon Rifkind has been around.

Rifkind was appointed to the Federal bench for the Southern District of New York by President Roosevelt in 1941.
He left in 1950 because, he said, he could not maintain "a
reasonable standard of living" on a judge's annual salary of
$15,000. Although *The Herald Tribune* mourned his de-
parture as the loss "of one of our ablest and hardest working
judges," Rifkind was not lost to public life. He was active
in civic affairs, politics, and court reform. His law firm, Paul,
Weiss, Rifkind, Wharton & Garrison, was one of the biggest
and most important in New York, and Judge Rifkind handled the biggest and most important cases. At the time he
was worrying about Bill Manchester for Mrs. Kennedy he
was worrying about another author, Ralph Nader, for General Motors. (Rifkind was assisted in this by Ted Sorensen,
who is a member of his firm.) Nader, the critic of automotive
safety, was suing General Motors for harassing him while he
prepared his book *Unsafe at Any Speed*.

Interestingly enough, Rifkind was involved with still a
third book case. In this one, though, he was fighting to get
the book published. It was *Pennsylvania—Birthplace of a
Nation*, by Sylvester K. Stevens, executive director of the
Pennsylvania Historical and Museum Commission. Helen
Frick, a daughter of the late Henry Clay Frick, the Pitts-
burgh coal baron, sued to prevent its publication because,
she said, it defamed her father, who died in 1919. Rifkind

said that if she was upheld it would be a violation of the
First Amendment guarantees of free speech and free press.

The meeting in *Look*'s suite at the Berkshire that brought
both Burke Marshall and Rifkind into the battle as cham-
pions of Mrs. Kennedy had been set up by Robert Kennedy,
although he did not attend it. Rifkind's presence was the
first sign that Mrs. Kennedy might take legal action. It was
a faint sign and it made no great impression, except to indicate to *Look* that either Bobby or Jackie was serious about
something.

The meeting began at 9 A.M. Besides Bill Attwood, Jack
Harding, the general counsel, was there for *Look*. In the
next few days, the Kennedy people came to think of Harding
as the hatchet man for Cowles, which was not entirely fair.
Harding is a pleasant, plump, middle-aged man, who happened to be absolutely certain that his side was right. He
was also cautious. When *Look* bought the serial rights to
The Death of a President, it received five Thermofax copies.
Harding locked one copy in the safe, where it would be
protected against fire, flood, and theft. Later, it was Harding
who hustled Manchester off the plane and told him to draw
up his chronology.

Marshall and Evan Thomas arrived at the meeting together, Thomas still in the role of publisher and friend of
the family. Then Rifkind and Bud Taylor, a lawyer in his
firm, got there. The meeting was neither as passionate nor
as unproductive as the meeting in Robert Kennedy's office a
few days before. It showed both sides exactly where they
were—apart. Marshall did most of the talking. Since it was
not a legal matter yet, and since he was there as a friend of
the family, he pleaded for Mrs. Kennedy's feelings. Harding
said that *Look* regarded the manuscript as Manchester's personal property, that it had negotiated an honorable contract
for it, and that Kennedy himself had been pleased when

Look acquired the rights to the serialization. He asked Marshall if Robert Kennedy was the spokesman for the Kennedy family and when Marshall appeared to hedge on the answer, Harding asked him what Kennedy had meant by his telegram saying that "members of the Kennedy family will place no obstacle in the way of publication."

Rifkind broke in and said that the telegram did not mean the family had approved publication of the manuscript. Simultaneously, he objected to the serialization and to publication on the anniversary of the assassination. It was apparent that the conference would not produce a meeting of minds and Rifkind concluded it by asking for a twenty-four-hour delay before anyone took further action. Harding said fine, although he did not know what was to happen next.

What did happen was the emergence of Jackie Kennedy as an active participant in the dispute. The next day she tried to call Gardner Cowles. He was out, but Harding heard of it and immediately called Rifkind. Lawyers know there is a certain protocol involved when there is a possibility that someone will sue someone else, and the protocol demands that a principal on one side of a possible suit does not casually call a principal on the other side. Harding wanted to know if Mrs. Kennedy had Rifkind's approval for calling Cowles. Rifkind said he could hardly stop her.

Mrs. Kennedy did reach Cowles at his home late that evening. She called him Mike, as all his friends do, and he called her Jackie. Mrs. Kennedy clearly did not want *Look* to publish the serialization at all, and she told Cowles that she was distressed by the whole thing. Cowles told friends later that he was a little baffled by the conversation, but that Mrs. Kennedy seemed to be mainly interested in getting *Look* to postpone the serialization. "November," she said, "is always a difficult time for the children and me."

Cowles indicated to Mrs. Kennedy that he would postpone the start of the serialization and he said that he would
talk to Cass Canfield of Harper & Row about putting off the
book publication. With regret, however, he declined an invitation to visit her in Hyannisport. Business elsewhere, he
said, would occupy him.

On the same day that Mrs. Kennedy called Gardner
Cowles, the first galley proofs from the printers were returned to Harper & Row. At this point no one on the Kennedy side was worried about the publisher; Evan Thomas
was still considered a Kennedy man and he was still receiving
suggestions from Pamela Turnure and Seigenthaler for revisions in the manuscript. Thomas has since said that he was
listening to the suggestions out of "courtesy" to the Kennedys
and that he was making a sincere effort to "minimize the
intense friction" that had developed. Certainly, he says, he
believed he was dealing with an "approved" manuscript.

Nonetheless, the Kennedys believed that Harper & Row
would make any changes they wanted, and they felt sure that
Thomas did not consider the manuscript approved. While
nothing is ever what it seems, Thomas did write a note to
Angie Novello that reinforced the view.

AUGUST 18

I am enclosing a letter from the president of the Book-of-
the-Month Club, which I hope you might show to Bob at
the proper time. Book-of-the-Month is, in our mind, a logical
extension of hardbound book publishing.

Their announcements are always in very good taste and
we could prevent them from any of the ordinary commercialization of the Manchester book—if and when we have
release for that book.

Back in July, when Congdon had distributed the manu-
scripts of *The Death of a President* to the six magazines, a

magazine editor had passed one through a Xerox machine and then surreptitiously sent a copy on to the Literary Guild. The Guild, in turn, had offered $225,000 for the right to distribute the book to its members. Under the contract Manchester had then with Harper & Row, he and the publisher would each have received a quarter of this and the Kennedy Library a half. Shortly after the Guild made its offer, however, the Book-of-the-Month Club submitted one for $250,000. Harper & Row accepted it, and Thomas says that, when he referred to a "release for that book" in his letter to Miss Novello, he meant a release for the sale to the Book-of-the-Month Club. If that is so, the Kennedys misread the message. Another letter that was sent at about the same time to "Ladies," meaning Pamela Turnure and Nancy Tuckerman, another secretary to Mrs. Kennedy, concluded:

> I think it is terribly important especially since I have told Manchester that while I cannot be the last word in his editing of the largely political material that I absolutely refuse to publish the book unless he pays exact attention to Pam's wishes on this other material.

Pam's wishes, however, were not Manchester's. For one thing, there was the problem of Miss Turnure's not being a professional editor or writer. Manchester had raised a structure, building scenes, creating moods, telling a story. It was simply too delicate a task to yank large sections of copy from the structure; it would have collapsed. Furthermore, even if Miss Turnure had been highly proficient at the job, Manchester was becoming less enchanted than ever with dealing with intermediaries. Which was unfortunate. On August 21, Manchester's neighbor, Dick Goodwin, called him in Maine and said that it was now official: he was speaking for Jackie and would represent her in her dealings with Manchester.

When Goodwin began this new assignment he had received a warning letter from Seigenthaler that said:

> Since you are now the "reader," I think I should alert you to the difficulties I had in dealing with Bill Manchester. He is a great writer, but in my opinion he has very bad judgment and is extremely sensitive when faced with the prospect of editing his work.
>
> About three weeks ago, I found that almost none of the several editing changes Ed Guthman and I thought should have been made had, in fact, been made.

Goodwin, however, did not talk of difficulties when he spoke to Manchester. He told him that Mrs. Kennedy would call him herself, and that she was distressed when she heard about the meeting in Robert Kennedy's office. Manchester says he was also told that Jackie had complete faith in him. Manchester waited in vain for a phone call from Mrs. Kennedy. A little perplexed, he wrote to Thomas: "Should any letter reach me from Jackie with specific suggestions I shall naturally reply immediately. This, however, is between you and me. I am reluctant to approve fresh changes in the approved manuscript."

Mrs. Kennedy, however, wasn't in much of a mood to talk or write to Manchester. She had renewed her invitation to Gardner Cowles to fly up to Hyannisport and again he had been unable to go. Then, on August 23, she called him again. This time she did not call him Mike; it was Mr. Cowles. She said she wanted him to come up to Hyannisport and she wanted him to bring a lawyer. If he did not come, she said, it would only be because he was afraid to face her.

Mrs. Kennedy said she had decided to stop the serialization and that it was absolutely imperative that she see Cowles the next day. Cowles, in turn, said it was hard for him to

leave New York on such short notice, but that he would do
so if he did not have to break an important luncheon date.
Fine, Mrs. Kennedy said. She told him that she would send
the *Caroline*, the family plane, to pick him up at the Marine
Air Terminal at La Guardia Airport. He would bring Jack
Harding; she would have Simon Rifkind.

Cowles and Harding presented themselves at the appointed
time and were flown to the Hyannis airport. People were
leaving Cape Cod after the summer holidays and the traffic
was heavy. Cowles and Harding had thought that a car would
be sent from the Kennedy compound to pick them up, but
instead Mrs. Kennedy herself showed up, full of good cheer
and in a Pucci dress.

The two men were driven to the compound. There was
iced tea and sandwiches, and Mrs. Kennedy took them on a
brief tour of the house and then announced, to their sur-
prise, that Robert Kennedy was also there. The Senator,
however, was in swimming. Rifkind, who had arrived earlier,
told Cowles that the Kennedys hadn't had a chance to confer
and asked if he and Harding would mind waiting for a few
minutes. Cowles said, of course not. He had never been to
Hyannisport before and he said that he and Harding would
wander down to the beach.

Cape Cod, the part that is away from exhaust fumes, sun-
tan oil, and fat ladies in shorts, is a nice place, scented by
saltwater, wild roses, honey locust, quahogs, and pine. It
had been a way station for the Kennedys since 1928 when
Joseph P. Kennedy bought a fourteen-room summer house
there with clapboards, shingles, and a roof with three gables.
The nine Kennedy children had played there, sailed there
and walked over to Turner's on Route 28 for ice cream.
When John and Robert grew up, houses were built for
them on each side of their father's in the 4.7-acre compound.
Robert's, a twelve-room cottage, got stuffed with children

and flowers from the Kennedy gardens. John's, an eleven-room place with five bathrooms, became the summer White House. Later, Stephen K. Smith, a Kennedy son-in-law built a summer home not far from the compound, while a mile and a half away, Senator Edward M. Kennedy bought a ten-room cottage on Squaw Island.

Tourists came down regularly on the Kennedy compound when Kennedy was President. They still do, of course, but during the Administration the police had to work harder to keep them away. Now the compound is quieter and the old summer White House is more truly a retreat. Jackie Kennedy has painted most of the inside yellow and hung it with sea-scapes and some of her own paintings and one by her husband, a primitive of the Riviera port of Villefranche.

Cowles and Harding strolled along the beach, pausing to admire one of Bob Kennedy's boys tossing a football. They paused so long that they got bored and strolled back to Mrs. Kennedy's cottage, where they found Mrs. Kennedy, the Senator, Burke Marshall, Rifkind, and Bud Taylor, his assistant, grouped around a brown metal table on a porch.

The conference began inauspiciously, with Rifkind saying it would be improper to serialize the book and the Senator suggesting that *Look* "tear up" the contract and forget about it. Cowles demurred, noting that *Look* had bought the manuscript with the full consent of the Kennedys. He would consider, he said, reducing the number of installments from seven to four, but he hardly saw how he could do much more than that. Mrs. Kennedy said that she simply couldn't understand why Cowles would proceed when she didn't want him to, and Rifkind interjected that he had advised Mrs. Kennedy that she could, if she wished, win a lawsuit. Harding said then, with some iciness, that he had told Cowles the same thing.

The conversation was going nowhere, and Kennedy sensibly suggested that they pass around the table and give everyone a chance to speak. He began by saying that Harding had misunderstood the messages he had sent to Manchester and Thomas. He said he had not approved Manchester's manuscript, which hadn't been revised to meet the objections that had been raised against it, and that anyway he had been speaking only for himself when he had sent the telegrams, not for Mrs. Kennedy.

"Bob doesn't represent me," Mrs. Kennedy explained. "He sort of protects me."

Harding recalled that *Look* had paid $665,000 for the serialization rights.

"If it's money I'll pay you a million," Mrs. Kennedy said coldly.

Harding said that it wasn't just money, and that *Look* thought it was a fine book.

Mrs. Kennedy pointed to him and said:

"You're sitting in the chair my late husband sat in."

Then she said she would demand that publication of both the book and the serialization be stopped.

"No," said the Senator, "not the book."

"Are you going to serialize?" Mrs. Kennedy asked Cowles.

"First, let me ask a question," Cowles said. "I sense an undercurrent of feeling that *Look* didn't act in good faith."

"*Look*," said the Senator, "acted in good faith."

"Yes, Mrs. Kennedy, we will publish," Cowles said.

Cowles would agree to only one real concession: delaying the publication date of the installments so that they would not appear during the anniversary of the assassination. He said that he would consider shortening the number of installments from seven to four, but that was all. Nonetheless, there was warmth all around when the meeting broke up. The Senator was friendly, and so was Jackie, who hugged Cowles and even smiled on Jack Harding. Everyone except Mrs. Kennedy flew back to New York then aboard the *Caroline,* along with a clutch of Kennedy relatives who had been in Hyannisport for a holiday. Ethel and Bob sat facing Cowles and Harding until Ethel left to join the relatives and was replaced by Rifkind. The Senator and Cowles did most of the talking, not about *The Death of a President,* however, but about "Suppose God Is Black," the piece by Kennedy that had just appeared in *Look.* Kennedy asked Cowles what he thought about it, and Cowles said it was just fine. The conversation continued while the *Caroline,* stacked up behind other planes because of delays on the ground, circled La Guardia. No one alluded to *The Death of a President* at all until the plane had landed. At the airport, Kennedy turned to Cowles and said:

"Mike, you're a publisher; see what you can do about this."

What Mike could do was to make a concession, but not a capitulation. Two days after the Hyannisport meeting, Harding wrote to Rifkind:

DEAR JUDGE RIFKIND:

In deference to the wishes of the Kennedy family, *Look* magazine has (1) postponed serialization of *The Death of a President* from the originally scheduled starting date of October 18, 1966 to January 24, 1967, and (2) shortened the number of installments from seven to four. Serialization will now start in *Look* with the January 24, 1967 issue and end with the issue dated March 7, 1967. Publication of the book by Harper & Row will occur on March 1, 1967, during the on-sale period of the last issue of *Look* containing material from the book. Announcement of the serialization will be issued next week.

Sincerely yours,
JOHN HARDING

A copy of the letter was sent to Senator Kennedy, apparently on the theory that he really was the spokesman for the family. Nevertheless, Rifkind called Harding at his home in Connecticut the next day and said he had been unable to reach either of the Kennedys to ask them what they thought of *Look*'s "proposal" to settle the dispute. Harding said *Look* was not making a proposal at all; it had made a decision, and the decision was final. *Look* would do no more.

There is a form that good lawyers follow when they square off and look the other guy in the eye. It demands that they adopt a position and stick to it, unyielding, never admitting that their client is in anything other than a position of perfect righteousness. Sometimes it demands that, for the record, the lawyer for the one side must fail to understand what the lawyer for the other side has just said.

So, on August 29 Rifkind wrote to Harding:

DEAR MR. HARDING:

I wish to confirm our telephone conversation on Saturday, in which I informed you that I would discuss with Mrs. Kennedy and Sen. Robert Kennedy the proposal contained in your letter of August 26 and would hope to have an answer to communicate to you not later than Tuesday, August 3, as to whether that proposal, or some modification thereof, would be acceptable to them.

So that there may be no further misunderstanding on the question of approval of text, I also want to re-emphasize that, regardless of any agreement which we may reach as to the form and timing of publication of the Manchester manuscript, neither Mrs. Kennedy nor Sen. Kennedy has approved any version of the text of that manuscript. Accordingly, any proposed publication of the manuscript, in any form, remains subject to the provisions of Paragraph 3 of the Memorandum of Understanding of March 26, 1964 between Robert F. Kennedy and William Manchester, which reads: "The completed manuscript shall be reviewed by

---

Mrs. John F. Kennedy and Robert F. Kennedy, and the text shall not be published unless and until approved by them."

Very truly yours,

SIMON H. RIFKIND

Harding, however, didn't have to wait until August 30 to hear if Mrs. Kennedy and the Senator would accept *Look*'s solution. The same day that Rifkind wrote the letter, the Senator called Cowles and said it wasn't good enough, that the postponement and the reduction in the number of installments were fine, but what really mattered was the manuscript itself. The corrections that he and Jackie wanted, he said, had to be made. Cowles said no.

The confusion that was creeping over everything then may be measured by Rifkind's subsequent request to Harding for a copy of the manuscript that *Look* had bought for the serialization. Seigenthaler, Guthman, and Pamela Turnure had read copies of the manuscript and commented on it. Evan Thomas had made flying trips to Washington, Los Angeles, and Nashville to discuss revisions. Arthur Schlesinger and Dick Goodwin read the manuscript, too. Nevertheless, none of the Kennedys or their advisers seemed to know what was in and what was out of anyone else's copy of *The Death of a President*. If Robert Kennedy had, in fact, approved the manuscript he was in the awkward position of not knowing what the hell he had approved.

There is a slender possibility that something could have been saved then. If a manuscript had been made quickly available to the Kennedys, if Dick Goodwin and Bill Attwood had sat down and gone over it, if positions on both sides were not allowed to calcify. It is, of course, the slenderest of possibilities. Harding, however, was in Florida, looking after another one of Gardner Cowles' far-flung outposts, and he did not receive Rifkind's letter until more than a week had passed. By then Cowles Communications had announced that it would serialize *The Death of a President,* and it had done so with a grand gesture, a full-page ad in *The New York Times* on the morning of September 1.

"The editors of *Look* announce the purchase of magazine publication rights to the most important book of 1967," the ad shouted, and it went on to quote what was to be the foreword to *The Death of a President.* The foreword told of Manchester's quest for the story, of the people he had seen, of the things he had done. The last paragraph said:

> Thanking everyone who helped me during two years of investigation is impossible. Nevertheless I must acknowledge my great debt to several of those without whom I should never have come to the end of this long journey. They are Mrs. John F. Kennedy; Robert F. Kennedy; Mrs. Lyndon B. Johnson; Eunice Shriver; Richard Cardinal Cushing; Theodore C. Sorensen; Arthur M. Schlesinger, Jr.; Richard N. Goodwin; McGeorge Bundy; Maj. Gen. Chester V. Clifton USA (ret.); Edwin O. Guthman; John Seigenthaler; Evelyn Lincoln; and Evan Thomas, who edited *Profiles in Courage* and now this book.

The view from Hyannisport was that the announcement was dreadful, and the acknowledgment worse: Jacqueline and Robert Kennedy were being credited with helping the author of a book they wanted to suppress. It was a touch of infamy. After Mrs. Kennedy filed suit and lawyers were striving to end the dispute out of court, the question of whom Manchester could acknowledge became a sticking point. Mrs. Kennedy insisted that neither her name nor that of any member of the Kennedy family could be used. For a while, in fact, her lawyers said that no one could be acknowledged. ("Not even my wife?" Manchester said. "Not even your wife," he was told.)

In the months ahead, *Look* publicized the serialization vigorously. The foreword was reproduced from the galley proofs with typographical errors and proofreader's corrections and sent into millions of homes as an inducement to subscribe to *Look*. It was accompanied by letters addressed to "Dear Friend" that were signed by Gardner Cowles (more infamy, Hyannisport thought), who noted that "Mrs. John F. Kennedy proposed to Mr. Manchester that he write this book" because she wanted "one complete, accurate account of those few days that stunned the entire world and changed the course of history."

A two-page ad in the magazine itself began: "This is the only book Jacqueline Kennedy asked to be written about her husband." It went on to note that "Mrs. Kennedy talked to the author for ten hours—about things she never discussed before or since." Another letter, this one signed by Bill Arthur, the editor of *Look*, began with a paragraph from the manuscript: "Spectator Charles Brend's [apparently Charles Brehm; the misspelling found its way into the book] five-year-old boy timidly raised his hand. President Kennedy smiled warmly. He raised his hand to wave back. There was a sudden, sharp, shattering sound." Then Arthur, too, went on to note that Mrs. Kennedy asked Manchester "to write the one complete, accurate account" of the assassination.

All the advertising handouts were true. Mrs. Kennedy had indeed initiated the project, but she is not a lady who lends her name easily to things, and certainly not to publicity for a book she wanted to suppress. Moreover, both she and Robert Kennedy believed that *Look* was sensationalizing the serialization. It was not a thing either of them took kindly to, and it drove them further away from any chance of an amicable settlement.

Manchester, meanwhile, was still in Maine, working on

the *Look* serialization and cherishing the hope that he and Mrs. Kennedy could work things out. He knew rumors of the dissension over the book were beginning to abound in the land and he was anxious. He wrote to Evan Thomas: "Please, for the time being, don't write any letters about the book or talk to anyone about it. I'm convinced Jackie and I can work this out."

So was Jackie. A few days later Goodwin called the author and said that Mrs. Kennedy wanted to see him in Hyannisport.

Seven

E<small>VAN</small> T<small>HOMAS</small> was not one for looking on the dark side of the moon. It was his belief that things could be set right if Jackie Kennedy granted Bill Manchester an audience instead of speaking to him through a network of intermediaries and repeatedly he had urged her to do so. Hindsight gives everyone great insight, of course, and hindsight here shows it was preposterous that Jackie Kennedy and Bill Manchester could settle anything.

Mrs. Kennedy wanted *Look* to abandon the serialization completely. She was offended by the advertisements, uneasy about the amount of money at stake, and wounded that Gardner Cowles himself was lending his name to the publicity campaign after she had asked him to drop the whole thing. Above all, she was mortified that bits and pieces of her personal life would appear in four issues of *Look*, at least eight million copies apiece, to be scattered throughout the land. It is a fact that *Look* was serious about presenting the installments with dignity and without lurid and dreadful display. But it is also a fact that *Look* was a magazine with a mass circulation and that it promoted the things it offered. It was difficult for Hyannisport to reconcile promotion with the thought of a dignified work of history that would be a monument to a slain man.

Speculation is frivolous, of course, but it is entertaining, too. What if, say, *American Heritage,* or *The American Scholar,* or *Sewanee Review* had bought the serialization? These are not magazines that find their way into dentists' offices, where they lie for months, idly thumbed by just anyone. They do not languish in pool halls, where they are shuffled through between games, or in barber shops, mixed in with comic books under the girlie calendars, or in drugstore racks next to *Photoplay,* where teen-agers can slurp Cokes and riffle the pages.

What if the serialization was to be read only by the academic community, not by women in housedresses who write letters to the editor saying that Jackie is entitled to her privacy and then hang slack-jawed on each last printed word about her? What if Jackie Kennedy's letter to her husband, for example, was not to be read by grocery clerks, bartenders, cops, hustlers, sailors, widows, fat ladies, caddies, teen-age girls, retired men, and American Legionnaires? Would it have made a difference to her? Sure.

Burke Marshall once said, "To have her personal life spread out, just like in a movie magazine, is distressing to her." Next to a passage in a *Look* galley proof about the last night that Mrs. Kennedy and her husband spent before the assassination, Dick Goodwin noted that "Mrs. JFK feels very strongly about this. Their sleeping arrangements, embracing, etc., will all be taken by *Modern Screen,* etc., sensationalized, cheapened. Asks if you will please take this out. This is just what got Arthur into trouble." The word "please" was underlined. Mrs. Kennedy is not equipped to be a public person, but she is, and she will continue to be as long as Kennedys run for office, which may be forever, as long as her presence can sway a single vote, as long as she is the repository for the nation's sadness over John Kennedy, and as long as she fails to convince anyone that, like Garbo, Lindbergh and J. D. Salinger, she really does want privacy.

Her invitation to Manchester to visit Hyannisport was extended with the understanding that Robert Kennedy would not be there and that there would be a calm discussion of the problem without "emotionalism." The last was a condition that neither she nor the author could really meet.

While Goodwin and Manchester had breakfast at the Stanhope Hotel in New York on the morning of September 7, Manchester took pains to draw up a precise agenda for the meeting. He said he wanted to carry back a proposal to *Look* that would settle the dispute, and a possibility, he believed, was that two of the installments could appear before the publication of the book and two could appear after it. A virtue of this was that *Look* would lose its exclusivity on the story. Therefore, it would not be so valuable a property and Manchester would be forced to pay back some of the $665,-000. He would be compensated for the loss by a share of the book royalties. Another virtue was that, if the book appeared before the serialization was completed, there would be fewer newspaper headlines. Everything would be in print at nearly the same time and not spread out over a couple of months.

It was an imaginative idea—and it wouldn't have settled anything. Mrs. Kennedy wanted the serialization erased, done away with. This was unacceptable to *Look* and to Manchester. If the serialization had to be published, then she wanted absolute assurance that it would not be offensive to her. Manchester could not give this assurance. He could only point out, and he did point out, that the manuscript had been read by Schlesinger, Goodwin, Guthman, Seigenthaler, Thomas, and four editors at Harper & Row and that he had "incorporated" their suggestions. He could only say, and he did

say, that he would consider new suggestions from Pamela
Turnure and Seigenthaler. Bill Manchester and Jackie Kennedy were far apart.

Manchester and Goodwin flew from La Guardia aboard
the *Caroline* and landed on Cape Cod at ten thirty in the
morning. Mrs. Kennedy, in sunglasses and a green miniskirt,
picked them up in a convertible and drove them to the compound. After iced tea on the porch, Jackie Kennedy, watched
by Manchester, Goodwin, and John Kennedy, Jr., water-
skied. Then Manchester and Mrs. Kennedy swam. Mrs. Kennedy, wearing skin diver's flippers, glided through the water.
Manchester, a bulky man, was less graceful. Moving heavily,
out of breath and with the shore still yards away, he thought:
"What if I drowned now? Would it end all the bickering
about the book?"

Recalling it later, Manchester saw nothing odd that he had
felt that way. Mrs. Kennedy had made a powerful impression
on him. "She's incredible," he said. "She's all woman. You've
got to spend a little time with her, to see her in the full spec-
trum. When she looks at you with those big eyes . . ." He left
the sentence unfinished. Gardner Cowles told a friend that
when Mrs. Kennedy invited him to Hyannisport it was as if
she were extending an invitation to the White House. To
refuse would be lese majesty. It is hard to deny Mrs. Kennedy. Manchester was trying with a certain desperation.

After swimming, there was lunch on the porch and the
beginning of a three-hour discussion among Mrs. Kennedy,
Goodwin, and Manchester. There was no one else except a
discreet Secret Service man, and he retreated. It ought to
have been a place and a time for a fruitful conference, but
it was not. Manchester insisted later that his proposals for
a settlement were never discussed, and most likely they
weren't. The conversation wandered.

Mrs. Kennedy said she disliked all the books that had been

written about her husband, including Arthur Schlesinger's. She said the behavior of Cowles and Harding was despicable, and she spoke of "all those rats at *Look.*" Nevertheless, she said, she still liked Manchester. "It's us against them," she said. "Your whole life proves you to be a man of honor." She said that her telephone number when she was a child was Rhinelander 4-6167, and she said that John, Jr., had undergone a tonsillectomy. She recalled that Manchester's first book, *Disturber of the Peace: The Life of H. L. Mencken,* had been given to her as a Christmas present, and that her husband had read it. She noted that she was still gracing the covers of movie magazines, and she discussed the birthday party that Bunny Mellon gave her in July. She said that here, on the same porch where they were sitting, Jack Harding had read aloud from the telegram Bob had sent in July and deliberately omitted an important phrase. She discussed the proposed monument to her husband in Arlington National Cemetery, and she wondered aloud when the public would lose its interest in the assassination. Robert Kennedy had been hostile to Manchester in Washington, she said, because he felt guilty, "like a little boy who knows he's done wrong." Then she said that she would "read every word" of *The Death of a President.*

"Everyone is telling me not to read it," she said. "I'm tougher than they think I am."

Mrs. Kennedy, however, was not as tough as she was desperate. Moreover, she was at a disadvantage in dealing with Manchester, who had one great commitment—to his book. Manchester may have broken the spirit, if not the letter, of his old agreement with Robert Kennedy; there is room to think that he did, although he has never indicated that he thought this was even remotely so, and he did not think so that day at Hyannisport. He told his lawyers and the executives at *Look* that he did not believe he could have been

THE MANCHESTER AFFAIR   133

absolutely honest with Mrs. Kennedy then because it "would have ruptured the thin membrane of civility to no purpose." Besides that, he said, he felt outmatched. Both Goodwin and Mrs. Kennedy were far more articulate than he.

Jackie Kennedy wanted Manchester to ally himself with her against *Look;* he did not tell her that he would not do it. Instead, he was evasive, and he said he would tell Gardner Cowles that Mrs. Kennedy did not consider Robert Kennedy's telegram a release for publication of the book. Cowles, of course, knew this, but Manchester's promise seemed to relieve Mrs. Kennedy.

Goodwin, who had far less of an emotional investment in the discussion than either Manchester or Mrs. Kennedy, said there was no approved version of *The Death of a President,* and the telegram from Robert Kennedy was a great misunderstanding. If Manchester pointed this out to Cowles, he said, *Look* would be forced to cancel publication of the serialization. If *Look* should plan to publish anyway, he said, Manchester could seek an injunction. Then, Goodwin said triumphantly, *Look* would be forced to sue Manchester, who would be supported by Mrs. Kennedy.

"Anyone who is against me will look like a rat unless I run off with Eddie Fisher," Mrs. Kennedy said.

"*Look* has no feelings," Goodwin declared. "They are only interested in selling magazines." Then he added:

"Of course, I would do the same if I were a magazine publisher."

Goodwin said that if the serialization were canceled, the loss to Manchester would be made up by a larger share of the book royalties. Again he asked Manchester if he would associate himself with Mrs. Kennedy against the magazine and the author replied:

"I'll see Cowles. I'll see what I can do."

Mrs. Kennedy suggested that Goodwin accompany Manchester when he spoke to Gardner Cowles. Manchester, who thought this a dreadful idea, said no, but that he would check back with Goodwin and tell him what had happened.

Manchester says he felt nothing but "despair" as Goodwin and Mrs. Kennedy drove him back to the airport. He knew they had agreed on nothing, and he could not understand why there was no opposition to the publication of the book. Goodwin had said that the book would be published "with dignity." Mrs. Kennedy said it would be done without "magazine hoopla and promotion." Manchester really didn't know what they were talking about, although they were not being inconsistent at all. They were confident that Harper & Row would make all the changes they wanted and that there would be an approved manuscript. In the end, ironically, it was Harper & Row, not *Look*, that brought on the suit. When the Kennedys were on the verge of surrendering to *Look*, when it seemed as if further pleas to the magazine were useless, Harper & Row reversed itself. This, Mrs. Kennedy thought, was too much. She filed suit.

There was one other piece of stage business at Hyannisport that day. Although Goodwin and Mrs. Kennedy seemed to oppose serialization, it was agreed that Goodwin would read the galley proofs and then indicate to Manchester what he thought were the objectionable parts. The arrangement was not arrived at lightly. During the three-hour conference, Goodwin called both Robert Kennedy's office and lawyer Rifkind's office for consultation. Manchester twice called Don Congdon, his agent. Manchester, to Goodwin's disappointment, had arrived at Hyannisport with neither the book nor the magazine proofs. Before he left, however, he told his agent to put the proofs on a plane for Hyannis that day and that Goodwin would pick them up at the airport. The plane arrived after Manchester left and Goodwin drove out to the airport to pick up the proofs. The proofs, however, were not there. The freight manager told Goodwin that indeed they had arrived, but that there had been a call from New York to return them. It is another of the small mysteries.

Meanwhile, back at *Look,* Jack Harding had just returned from his business trip. Rifkind's letter asking for a copy of the manuscript had been languishing in his office for more than a week, and to an extent it had been superseded by events. Nevertheless, Harding replied at length:

SEPTEMBER 8, 1966

DEAR JUDGE RIFKIND:

Supplementing our recent telephone conversations, and with particular reference to your letter of August 31st, it is my understanding that the copy of the manuscript William Manchester furnished to you yesterday through Richard Goodwin is substantially identical to the manuscript which was submitted to LOOK Magazine and others on July 18, 1966 for bids for first serial rights therein. In order to remove any doubts, I am willing, as I told you earlier today, to have your representative come over to our offices and check your manuscript against ours in the presence of one of my associates.

In this connection, although our respective positions have been quite fully expressed on several occasions over a period of approximately four weeks, I cannot let go unchallenged the statement regarding approval of text contained in your letter of August 29th. It is now, and always has been, LOOK Magazine's position that (1) the text of the manuscript of July 18th in which it purchased first serial rights was approved by Robert F. Kennedy, acting for all members of the Kennedy family, including Mrs. John F. Kennedy, and (2) the sale of first serial rights in the manuscript at this time was similarly approved.

Without going into great detail, let me very briefly repeat the chronology of events. On *March 25, 1966,* the first complete manuscript was delivered by Mr. Manchester to Senator Kennedy. Five "readers" were designated to review the manuscript, with John Seigenthaler and Edwin O. Guthman representing Senator Kennedy. Substantial revisions were suggested by the readers and adopted by Mr. Manchester. Finally, on Thursday, *July 14, 1966,* Mr. Seigenthaler telephoned Evan Thomas that the last revision—which is the July 18th manuscript submitted to LOOK, of which you have a copy—was acceptable to Senator Kennedy and the Kennedy family and that magazine submission could begin. On *July 17th,* Mr. Manchester wrote Senator Kennedy referring to this approval as follows:

"Naturally I was pleased to hear from Evan Thomas Thursday that you agree with us about the desirability of publishing the book the first week in January 1967, preceded by the usual serialization, and that you are writing me to that effect. I was especially touched by your reason for approval; President Kennedy's opinion of me and my work. As you know, that is a prize I cherish above all others, and I shall continue to try to be worthy of it.

"The book benefited enormously from the suggestions of the five readers: Evan, John Seigenthaler, Ed Guthman, Arthur Schlesinger and Dick Goodwin. John and Ed were especially generous of their time and perceptive in their comments. Because of them, the manuscript is tighter, stronger, and more responsible. In writing it I attempted to keep a taut rein on my own feelings. Inevitably they sometimes intruded, however, and the readers were, therefore, as invaluable as they were necessary. Of course, Evan and I will continue to scrutinize the text carefully, to make certain that no abridgement violates the version we've all agreed upon."

Copies of this letter were sent at the same time to John Seigenthaler, Ed Guthman and Evan Thomas. On *July 18th,* copies of the approved manuscript were sent out to elicit bids for first serial rights. *The written approval* referred to in the July 17th letter was given by Senator Kennedy in (1) a letter to Evan Thomas dated July 28th and (2) a telegram to William Manchester on July 29th. These dates are significant since bids for first serial rights had to be in the hands

of Mr. Manchester's agent by 5:00 P.M. on July 29th. On
July 29th, Mr. Manchester wrote Senator Kennedy, thanking
him for the telegram and assuring the Senator that "I can
guarantee you that it will be handled with dignity and taste,
and without the faintest tinge of sensationalism. I can guarantee it because I'm the man who will be making the decisions." On the same date, Mr. Manchester also wrote to Mrs.
John F. Kennedy reporting on the completion of the manuscript, etc.

Prior to the submission of any bid for first serial rights
in the manuscript, LOOK's Washington Editor, Warren
Rogers, contacted Senator Kennedy on *July 27, 1966* and
advised him of LOOK's interest in serializing the book,
"THE DEATH OF A PRESIDENT." Mr. Rogers asked
Senator Kennedy if the latter had read the Manchester manuscript and the Senator replied that he had not and was not
going to read it but that John Seigenthaler and Ed Guthman
had read it for him and were acting as his "agents." Senator
Kennedy, when asked what his personal view would be of
LOOK's acquiring serialization rights as opposed to other
bidding magazines, stated that his attitude was "favorable"
and suggested that Mr. Rogers, if he wished, might call John
Seigenthaler about the serialization. Promptly after the submission of LOOK's bid and the acceptance of such bid by
Mr. Manchester's agent, Senator Kennedy was advised on
Saturday, July 30th that LOOK had acquired the serial rights.
At that time, Senator Kennedy also expressed satisfaction
that LOOK would be doing the serialization.

LOOK Magazine purchased from William Manchester first
serial rights in "THE DEATH OF A PRESIDENT." Mr.
Manchester, at all times since the original memorandum
agreement of March 26, 1964, retained such rights and it
was always contemplated by the parties to that memorandum
that there would be a "sale of serial option rights to a responsible publisher." The manuscript in which LOOK bought
first serial rights—the July 18th manuscript—had been approved by Senator Kennedy acting for the Kennedy family
and serialization at this time had been similarly approved,

as clearly evidenced by the correspondence and particularly the letter and telegram of July 28th and July 29th, respectively. We have, as I advised you on August 26th, changed our plans—both as to timing and form of serialization—in deference to the wishes of the Kennedy family. We intend to present this material in LOOK Magazine as one of the most important historical documents of our time. To avoid any possibility that in serialization incidents might be taken out of context or summarized in any way which might distort the facts, we are having every page of every installment in LOOK Magazine checked by Mr. Manchester who, as the author, is in the best possible position to guarantee against any distortion. We also know that both Mrs. John F. Kennedy and Senator Kennedy have complete confidence in, and respect for, Mr. Manchester's ability as an historian and reporter.

Harding's final fillip, that he knew of the Kennedys' respect for Manchester as a historian and a reporter, was his own indulgence, of course. Harding had a fair idea that the Kennedys wished they had never heard of William Manchester, but he was feeling a rising personal pique with the whole business, and it had not been allayed by Manchester's account of the meeting at Hyannisport.

A few days later Manchester wrote to Mike Land, who was now in the last throes of putting together the serialization for *Look*. "As you know," Manchester said, "the agreement between me and *Look* provides that the Kennedys may designate representatives to advise the author, the purpose of this provision being to assure the condensation of the manuscript is in keeping with the spirit of the book." Therefore, Manchester asked, would he please pass on an extra set of proofs of the serialization so that Dick Goodwin could examine them?

Land passed on the galleys to Manchester and the letter to Harding. Manchester's interpretation of the contract between

Cowles and himself made the general counsel of Cowles nervous. He had no objection to the Kennedys or their people examining the galleys, but he damn well wanted everyone to know that no one was going to censor anything. Manchester had told Jackie Kennedy that he had "tied the tightest strings in publishing history" to his book, which may have been true. The strings, however, did not include the right to excise material from the manuscript. While *Look* had allowed far more control over the manuscript than *Life,* for example, it was insistent that it get what it had paid for: the right to use any 80,000 words of a 320,000-word manuscript. Harding wrote:

SEPTEMBER 16, 1966

DEAR BILL:

A copy of your letter to Mike Land dated September 10 has just come to my attention. Frankly, I am very disturbed by it because it does not summarize correctly the terms of our agreement covering the above book and therefore could be misleading particularly to persons not familiar with the agreement.

Under our agreement dated August 11 Cowles purchased rights in a specific approved manuscript—the manuscript submitted to LOOK on July 18—and that is the controlling document. At no time have we ever agreed that the LOOK articles must be "in keeping with the spirit of the book." Nor have we ever agreed that the Kennedys might designate "representatives to advise the author ... to assure that spirit of the book." We did give you specific right of approval of the installments to be certain that in the condensation there would be no erroneous change of any factual material or change of the meaning of the material as contained in the approved manuscript. This same right was extended to Mrs. John F. Kennedy and Senator Robert F. Kennedy through you in the event that they wish to check the LOOK articles for the sole purpose of being assured that in our editing we had not changed the meaning of any of the material taken from the approved manuscript. Just so that these two provisions will be fresh in your mind, let me quote them:

"In the preparation of the LOOK Magazine articles, COWLES shall be entitled to use whatever material from the manuscript which COWLES may select and to omit whatever material it may desire, but may not add any other material thereto without the approval of AUTHOR. However, so that there can be no question *as to COWLES' having erroneously changed any factual material, or having substantially changed the meaning of any of the material, as contained in the manuscript, by such editing, cutting, etc., for the LOOK articles,** COWLES agrees to submit first proofs and final photostats of each page of each LOOK article for prior approval to AUTHOR in care of AGENT, 30 Rockefeller Plaza, New York, New York, and COWLES will not publish same without such approval."

"If AUTHOR timely notifies COWLES that Mrs. John F. Kennedy or Senator Robert F. Kennedy similarly desire the right to review said material *to determine whether the LOOK articles have substantially changed the meaning of any of the material contained in the manuscript,** COWLES agrees to submit same to them through AUTHOR."

We will not accept any censorship of the LOOK articles by anyone and I am sure that as the responsible author of this historic document you will also strongly resist any attempt to censor the material. We have no way of knowing what editing will be done on the book version and, of course, we at LOOK are not concerned with that.

I understand that you will be in the office next week, Bill, and if you have any questions about this letter, I would appreciate your checking with me at that time.

With best regards

A week or so after Harding's reply to Manchester, Mrs. Kennedy was on the phone again with Gardner Cowles, very politely asking him if he could meet with Goodwin that day.

* Italics added.

The bitterness that was evident in their Hyannisport meeting, Cowles thought, had passed. Nevertheless, Cowles expected her to thank him for delaying the series and shortening the number of installments. She did not, and it annoyed him.

"I had expected to get some word of thanks," he says. "I never got any."

He did, however, agree to meet Goodwin, whom he saw that afternoon. Harding was there, too, and when Goodwin also failed to acknowledge what he considered to be generosity by *Look*, Harding, too, got annoyed. "I told Goodwin how I felt," he says simply. It was another meeting that began poorly and ended the same way.

While they discussed changes in the copy, Cowles asked Goodwin if he had spoken to Manchester about them. Goodwin said no, and Cowles told him that *Look* would make no changes without the author's consent. Furthermore, he said, *Look* would agree to make no more than factual corrections, although it would consider suggestions for other changes.

Although *Look* had bought the right to use 80,000 words in the manuscript, it decided that a serialization of 60,000 words, four installments at 15,000 words apiece, would be the most effective length for magazine purposes. Goodwin had received the galleys for the first and second installments on September 13. There was an understanding that he would pass them back to Manchester, who would give them to *Look* within five days. Nevertheless, six days later, Manchester told Bill Arthur, the editor of *Look*, that the galleys had not been returned. Goodwin, he said, had dropped out of sight and efforts to reach him by phone "in Massachusetts, Connecticut, New York, and Washington were unavailing."

A few days later, however, Goodwin materialized for the meeting with Cowles and Harding, and several days after that the galley proofs for the first and second installments, both precisely marked with requests for deletions, were returned to *Look*.

In the first installment, Goodwin had requested a cut of only 288 words. In the second installment, he wanted a cut of only 270 words. Nearly all of the deletions dealt with Mrs. Kennedy and nearly all of them touched on things that were highly personal—for example, a letter she had written to her husband, a description of the sleeping arrangements at Fort Worth. A few were frivolous: a reference to her searching for wrinkles as she sat in front of a mirror ("She must be very vain," Gardner Cowles said solemnly when he saw the editing), a request that Mrs. Kennedy be "fumbling" not "fidgeting." One or two were marginal, midway between politics and personalities, such as a revision in a quote by Mrs. Kennedy in which she spoke about Governor John Connally, Jr., of Texas.

By and large, there was a feeling at *Look* that the requested revisions were understandable. Indeed, there was some astonishment that, after all the phone calls, the meetings at Hyannisport, the letters and lawyers and tears and swearing, the Kennedys wanted so little. Subsequently, the copy checkers at *Look,* the people who try to verify each fact in an article, worked a little harder. Manchester planned to leave for London next month and they wanted to finish before his departure. General Counsel and Vice-President Harding chose to enter a hospital for an operation. Editor Bill Arthur took the vacation that he had deferred and went to the Middle East. Senior Editor Mike Land began to think about the book he was doing with Lee Harvey Oswald's brother, and Gardner Cowles was left musing about the ways of Jacqueline Kennedy. It was a respite, and it ended officially on the night that Editor-in-Chief Bill Attwood attended a party at the home of John Gunther.

Attwood, the loyal John Kennedy man, had never been

really involved in the negotiations over *The Death of a President*. He had been a *Look* correspondent for years before Kennedy appointed him an Ambassador, but he had returned only recently to be editor-in-chief. He hadn't been in touch with the controversy about the serialization until the meeting in mid-August at the Berkshire Hotel with Burke Marshall and Simon Rifkind.

Now, like the other *Look* editors, he thought that the problems were solved. At the party he found out otherwise. Bobby Kennedy was there and so was Arthur Schlesinger. Attwood walked over to Kennedy and said:

"Well, everything seems to be OK now."

"What makes you think everything is OK?" Kennedy said and walked away.

Then Attwood approached Schlesinger, who said:

"There will never be another Kennedy by-line or my by-line in *Look*."

Attwood was mystified, and in time his mystification gave way to bitterness. "The whole affair," he says, "was senseless. Jackie Kennedy could have had anything she wanted if she hadn't sued."

Attwood did not know it on the night he confronted Bobby Kennedy and Schlesinger, but the week before, the Senator and a clutch of his advisers had seriously debated the possibility of a suit against *Look* after they had examined the third installment of the serialization. Manchester had passed the proofs for the installment on to Goodwin at the end of September and told him, he says, that the five-day agreement on their return was still in effect.

By the first week in October, however, Goodwin had kept the proofs eleven days, and one afternoon, Manchester, determined to rescue them, walked from his office in the Wesleyan University library over to Goodwin's glass-walled office in the Center for Advanced Studies. (There is a picture of John F.

Kennedy there, too; it shows the President and Goodwin examining the bill that was to result in the creation of the Peace Corps.) The author asked Goodwin's secretary if Goodwin were available. He was not, and Manchester explained that he only wanted to pick up the proofs that Goodwin supposedly had left for him.

Goodwin, who is a man of many papers, is as likely to file things on the sofa or the floor as in a filing cabinet, and he had left the proofs lying about where Manchester could see them. The author picked them up, thanked the secretary, and left. "There was never a five-day agreement on the proofs," Goodwin says. "Manchester just took them." It was another of the small misunderstandings.

A little earlier, the proofs had been the focal point of a prolonged meeting in Senator Kennedy's apartment in New York. Until then the assortment of people who had been advising and representing the Kennedys on things to do with *The Death of a President* had not been gathered in a group. John Seigenthaler and Ed Guthman had been on the phone constantly. Pierre Salinger had written a memo about how it all began. Ted Sorensen had conferred with Simon Rifkind, and Burke Marshall had presented himself for a couple of conferences. Goodwin at various times had been in touch with nearly everyone. On a Thursday, however, along with the Senator himself and a few lesser known members of his camp such as James Greenfield, a former State Department official, and John Douglas, a son of Paul Douglas, the former Senator from Illinois, they drew together to consider one great question: Should we sue?

No, they decided. Robert Kennedy could not be put in the position of wanting to suppress a book. Jackie Kennedy would find it intolerable if she were forced to appear as a witness in a trial. Then, too, there was some feeling that *Look* might yield on the changes. Certainly, it was thought, Harper & Row would. The meeting lasted nearly three hours and then broke up into a series of smaller meetings that ended on a Tuesday night with dinner at 21. Later the Kennedys speculated that news of the decision not to sue reached what they called "the other side" and strengthened its resolve not to make changes in the manuscript. (During the days of the suit, "the other side," very seriously, got to calling the Kennedys "the other side," too. It was like the Union and the Confederacy, the Bolsheviks and the Mensheviks, the Crusaders and the Saracens—two great adversaries.) In fact, *Look,* Harper & Row, and Bill Manchester knew all about the meeting and the decision not to sue. They solemnly deny, however, that the knowledge led them to be more forceful in trying to keep the manuscript intact.

Besides weighing the merits of a suit, Robert Kennedy and his advisers had pondered the *Look* serialization and decided that the third installment was the most damaging. This told of the flight from Dallas to Washington, the exchange between Robert Kennedy and Lyndon Johnson on where the new President should take the oath, the tawdry scene in Parkland Hospital when a county official tried to block the removal of Kennedy's body, and J. Edgar Hoover's conduct toward Robert Kennedy after he learned of his brother's death.

In none of these things did the Kennedy partisans come off really badly. They behaved with something less than generosity to Lyndon Johnson on the flight aboard Air Force One, according to the account published in *Look,* but to nonpolitical readers it hardly seemed like a dreadful portrayal. Johnson himself was written about with some sympathy, and he was said to feel slighted by the Kennedys. The real villain in the installment was probably the city of Dallas.

There is at least a possibility that distrust had been building up against *The Death of a President* among Robert Kennedy's advisers and that they could not shake themselves free of it. Manchester admits that he found it difficult to prevent his own attitudes from interfering with the job of objective reporting. He told Mrs. Kennedy, "I tried desperately to suppress my bias." He told Robert Kennedy his feelings "sometimes intruded." He was right, and there was agreement among the first readers of the manuscript that Manchester had been unfair to Lyndon Johnson and his Texas colleagues in the unexpurgated version of *The Death of a President.*

There was the deer-hunting incident, of course, and there was an episode in which an assistant to President Kennedy appeared to be blaming Lyndon Johnson and the Texans aboard Air Force One for the assassination. Actually the assistant, who is a volatile man, was doing nothing of the sort, but the quote attributed to him by Manchester could have been misconstrued. The quote was taken out in the early editing, but the Kennedys' wariness toward *The Death of a President* lingered on.

It is easy to understand and to sympathize with Mrs. Kennedy's objections to Manchester's use of much of the personal material. It is also easy to understand the objections of the Senator and his colleagues to the political and historical matter. It is, however, far less easy to sympathize with them.

They believed that Manchester was breaking his word by not making all the changes they wanted. They believed they had every right to ask for these changes, and they probably believed that the picture of Lyndon Johnson was unfair and that in attempting to change it they were doing something wholly decent. Nonetheless, there is an indictment: the Senator and his advisers allowed practical politics to determine what the historical record would show. They did not raise the question of truth or falsity in many of their objections. They wanted a truly authorized history, perhaps not an inaccurate one, but one that just omitted part of the history. Perhaps the advisers were being overzealous. Perhaps they were only capricious, but certainly they were wrong.

Look received the proofs for the third installment with the requested changes on October 7. The Kennedys wanted a total deletion of 2,737 words. When the proofs of the fourth and last installment were returned, there was a request that 3,177 words be cut. The total of the affected material in all four installments was 6,472 words, with slightly less than half of them dealing with matters that had political and historical implication.

John Seigenthaler said later that he had handled the manuscript just as he would "any story that came into my newsroom." In a note to *Look*, Goodwin said that the request for trims was just "normal editing."

Seigenthaler is a good man, but there is room to doubt that, as editor of the Nashville *Tennessean*, he would have approached a story in his newsroom in the same spirit as the Kennedy advisers approached the editing in the *Look* serialization. For one thing, they objected to the exchange between Kennedy and Johnson on where the new President should take the oath. They objected to the description of J. Edgar Hoover telling Robert Kennedy that his brother had died. They objected to comments that Manchester himself made about Johnson, without denying their accuracy. They objected to references to the discord between Johnson and Robert Kennedy, and they objected to the characterization of Dallas as a city of extremism.

On the proofs, the editing that dealt with Mrs. Kennedy was marked by a circle or an ellipsis. The editing that dealt with political material was marked with precise squares or rectangles, sometimes marked with the word "cut."

Therefore, there was never much question about what was regarded as political and what was regarded as personal, and only in a few cases, such as Mrs. Kennedy's quote about Governor John Connally did they overlap. The Kennedy editors say that in making the distinction between the two kinds of editing so apparent they were trying to ease the task of the *Look* editors who were charged with revising the serialization. In fact, it did not; it complicated it. The Kennedy colleagues say they had set up a system of priorities: the passages dealing with Jackie had to go, or they had to be at least revised; the political passages were secondary. These, they say, were things that they hoped would be changed.

The effect of the two sets of changes, the political and the personal, was to make the *Look* editors and Manchester suspicious. At least one *Look* executive wondered aloud if the Senator was using Mrs. Kennedy's request for changes as a guise to secure his own. Under this theory, Goodwin, who is every inch political, was never working for Jackie; it was always Bobby. Later, after the suit was filed, a number of stories were passed around about Manchester's emotional state. Most of them began in the Kennedy camp, and their effect was to discredit both Manchester and the book. This, some people on "the other side" thought, was Kennedy's way of casting doubt on the political revelations in *The Death of a President*.

There is some truth to all of these things. Goodwin was working for both Bobby and Jackie. In the up-tight world of the Kennedys, everyone is expected to have identical interests. Goodwin was looking after both of them. There were stories put around about Manchester's emotional state that gave Bobby and Jackie the benefit of the doubt as to who was right and who was wrong in the dispute. It may be a mistake to think, as a few columnists did, however, that the Kennedys' friends set out to conduct a whispering campaign.

They didn't have to. The fact is that Robert Kennedy has many people connected with him. They popped up all over the place. Many of them knew reporters and magazine writers. Many of them *were* reporters and magazine writers. Manchester, *Look,* and Harper & Row were simply outnumbered.

Eight

———— ～～ ————

INVITATIONS to Hickory Hill, Robert Kennedy's home in Virginia, are not extended lightly. Few of the Senator's staff have been there except to work. Robert Kennedy cherishes his family and his privacy more than is generally realized, and he does not deliberately mix them in with business. For Hickory Hill, then, it was a grave matter when Bill Manchester arrived there on October 10 for his last confrontation with a Kennedy.

For months the Senator had been deep in issues, aligning himself with good government people in New York and liberals in Congress. Moreover, he was in demand as a personality. By August he had received some one hundred invitations to speak for candidates in the November elections, and he had said that he would campaign in at least eight states. He also enlisted in the movement to save the police Civilian Review Board, and in the fall he spoke from dozens of street corners in New York City. Neither the board nor the Democrats did well in November, but it was hardly his fault. He had drawn crowds and applause nearly everywhere.

The Senator must have found *The Death of a President* a

wholly unwelcome intrusion when he met with Bill Manchester. Nonetheless, he was on his best behavior, and so was
Manchester. Neither wanted the bitter and fruitless debate
that had destroyed their last meeting in Washington. Dick
Goodwin, who accompanied Manchester to Hickory Hill
that day, recalls the confrontation as amicable. Manchester
says it was not angry, but not really amicable, either. As in
all things in the dispute, the recollections depend on whether
you were interested in one side or the other.

Everyone agrees, however, that Goodwin and Manchester
flew to Washington on October 10 and were at Hickory Hill
from about five thirty to seven thirty in the evening. Goodwin says that it was a pleasant time—"dinner with Ethel and
the kids." Manchester says that Kennedy appeared to be
reconciled to the *Look* serialization, and that he wanted
changes primarily in the hardcover book. These, he said, he
wanted in deference to Mrs. Kennedy. Furthermore, Manchester insists, Kennedy agreed that the third installment in
Look, the one his advisers thought was the most damaging to
himself and to President Johnson, was factually correct and
a contribution to history.

Although Manchester recalls Kennedy as being reconciled
to the serialization, he also says the Senator told him he
would approach Gardner Cowles again and ask him to accept
the changes that Mrs. Kennedy wanted. If the personal
changes were made, he said, he would abandon all thoughts
of court action. Robert Kennedy does not usually bluff, but
there was an element of it here. He had already decided
that a suit was out of the question.

The Hickory Hill meeting had begun with a dip in the
Senator's swimming pool, which Manchester found discon-
certing. For one thing, it was October and he was cold. For
another, he says, Kennedy would ask a question, submerge

and pop up behind him, his hair streaming over his face. Then he would ask another question before Manchester could answer the first one and submerge again. "It was weird," Manchester says. (Kennedy had used the swimming pool for tactical purposes before. A reporter who was at Hickory Hill says he once asked Kennedy a question that he did not want to answer. He says Kennedy jumped in the pool, swam its length underwater, emerged on the other side, and, without once turning his head, climbed out and walked into the house. The reporter says he folded his notebook and left.)

As he had been with Jacqueline Kennedy at Hyannisport, Manchester was evasive with her brother-in-law, who wanted him to actively associate himself with the request for changes.

"Bill," Kennedy said between submersions, "you have the vagueness of a genius."

After swimming, Kennedy and Manchester, along with Goodwin, went into the house. Ethel Kennedy supervised dinner, and the three men discussed, among other things, speech writing. Manchester recalls that Kennedy introduced the subject. Goodwin says that Manchester did. Manchester says he felt that Kennedy was holding out the promise of becoming a speech writer in a new Administration, of establishing himself with a man who would be President. "Nonsense," Goodwin says, "this guy said he wanted to write a speech for Bob on academic freedom and that he had all this material, stuff stacked up to here. He volunteered to do it."

Dinner, anyway, was not controversial. (Ethel Kennedy and one of the children discussed the theory of evolution.) Nonetheless, there seems to have been an unease on Manchester's part. When he and Goodwin left and flew back to New York, Manchester insisted that they sit in separate sections of the plane. He wanted to think, he says. According to the Senator, before Manchester left he agreed to make the changes sought by Mrs. Kennedy. If this is so, the author had much to think about.

If Kennedy suspected, however, that Manchester was ready to capitulate, he was wrong. A week after the meeting at Hickory Hill, he called Manchester and invited him to another meeting, this one in New York. *Look,* he said, was sensationalizing the account. He had heard, for instance, that one installment told of the President and his wife going to bed together. Manchester declined the invitation to the meeting, and assured Kennedy that *Look* was not sensationalizing anything.

Manchester also assured the Senator that he would pass the galley proofs for the book on to Goodwin and that he would at least consider the changes. He did this on October 26, and it was followed by another of the small misunderstandings. Manchester says he told Goodwin that he must have the proofs back in two weeks—by November 10. The author, who is a firm believer in memorandums, had met with the executives of Harper & Row and one of their lawyers earlier and had drawn up a memorandum with six points, the third of which said:

"If the author has heard nothing from Goodwin in two weeks, he will write the publisher and advise him to proceed with the book."

Now, two weeks after he had given Goodwin the proofs, Manchester wrote the publisher to say that he had not heard from him and that he thought they ought to go ahead and publish. He had not heard from Goodwin, however, because Goodwin was in Italy. He says it was not quite a secret that he was there, and that Manchester, his neighbor and colleague at Wesleyan, knew all about it. Upon such things did the argument feed.

Bobby Kennedy, meanwhile, was nervous. Also vexed. Early in November he called Gardner Cowles and requested another meeting. Cowles was amenable, if not eager, and it was agreed that they would get together on November 16. Between then and November 16, which was also the day Manchester was to sail for London, there was a stillness. Seigenthaler and Pamela Turnure passed on requests for thirty new changes to Harper & Row, *Look* pressed ahead in its promotion campaign, and Manchester packed his bags. He also caught a cold, not much of one, but a cold. It got to be terribly important.

On November 15, Manchester and his wife arrived in New York for a cocktail party with the editors and executives of *Look* and Harper & Row. Don Congdon, Manchester's agent, was also there, and it was intended to be a social occasion. No one had met Julia Manchester before and the eve of Manchester's departure for London seemed to call for something special. No one was very happy about anything, of course, but the editors wanted to show solidarity with their author, and their author wanted to look only on friends, certainly on no Kennedy, no Kennedy representative, no Kennedy associate. The man who had adored John Kennedy had had it with the rest of the family, and to avoid them and to avoid any reporters who might be lurking about he checked into the Berkshire Hotel in the name of Don Congdon.

Evan Thomas had suggested to Manchester that they meet the next morning, the day of his departure for London, to go over the book galleys. Thomas called for a breakfast meeting at 7 A.M. Manchester reminded Thomas about the cocktail party and said that after it he intended to sit up all night to work on the book galleys. It is characteristic of Manchester, who is not a breakfast-eating type who keeps regular hours and frets about his health, that he said seven o'clock was too early. But seven thirty, he said, would be fine.

After the cocktail party, Manchester settled down to a bleak night of work, revising and correcting the Harper & Row galleys. The *Look* suite, Room 1704, is comprised of two bedrooms with a sitting room in between. Manchester worked in the sitting room until seven, when he took a bath. Then, with a brassy taste in his mouth, a sheaf of galleys under his arm, and a dim happiness because soon he would be in England, he went downstairs for breakfast with Thomas.

Manchester greeted the editor, ordered coffee, and began to talk about the book. He was interrupted by the arrival of Burke Marshall and Dick Goodwin, who pulled out chairs and sat down. Goodwin, who does not lack for *chutzpah,* said cheerfully:

"Well, it looks as if we'll all be sailing on the *Queen Mary.*"

The taste in Manchester's mouth got brassier.

There is a legend that when Burke Marshall and Bobby Kennedy first met they stared at each other for five minutes before either man spoke. Marshall is not much for small talk. With Manchester he got right down to business.

"If Mike Cowles agrees to new changes will you approve?"

Manchester said yes.

"Will you associate yourself with further changes?"

Manchester fled. (A problem in dealing with the Kennedys, he says, is that when you start to retreat you continue to retreat.) Trailed by Thomas, he dashed into the elevator, arose, and hurried down the hall to Suite 1704.

"You told them I'd be there," he told Thomas.

"No, no," the editor said.

"You betrayed me."

"Bill, I didn't betray you."

It was dreary and desperate, and it was broken off only when the doorbell rang. Manchester and Thomas stared at each other, and it rang again, and then again.

A voice called out.

"Bill, are you in there?"

Incredible, Manchester thought. It sounds like Robert Kennedy.

"Bill, I know you're in there."

It *was* Robert Kennedy.

"I didn't betray you," Thomas whispered hoarsely.

Ring. Then a pounding of fist against wood.

"Bill, Bill, I know you're in there."

The second of the two bedrooms in the *Look* suite was occupied by a mild and pleasant man called Bob Jones, who is the editor of *Family Circle,* which is also a Cowles publication. Jones peered out from his bedroom door, saw two men sitting in the living room, and decided that the sensible thing to do was to answer the doorbell.

"Tell him I'm not here," Manchester said.

Jones opened the door. Kennedy looked hard at Jones.

"If they don't want to see us, just tell us that."

Jones padded back to Manchester.

"Tell him I've got to see my lawyer."

Jones padded back to the door.

"They just don't want to see you."

Kennedy, Goodwin, and Marshall left. They walked around the corner to the Waldorf. They sat down on the lobby stairs.

"Well," said Kennedy, "what do we do now?"

While Kennedy was despondent, Manchester was unnerved. In some shock he called Don Congdon, who, in turn, called Jack Harding at *Look.*

"What should I do?" Congdon asked.

"Get Manchester on the ship as soon as possible," Harding replied.

Congdon did. Months later, a photographer who happened to be on board the *Queen Mary* that day recalled "a big guy, very nervous, who had a bad case of chapped lips. He looked as if he would fall down any minute." It was Manchester.

Kennedy had attempted a tactical maneuver that morning, and it had failed. The night before, while Manchester worked over the proofs in his hotel room, the Senator and Gardner Cowles had attended a dinner party given by Mrs. Douglas Dillon, wife of the former Secretary of the Treasury. Kennedy, sitting to Mrs. Dillon's right, told Cowles, sitting to her left, that he wanted to bring Goodwin to the meeting they had scheduled the next day. Cowles said this was fine, and that he would bring Harding.

Persuasion, however, had failed on Cowles before, and the Senator wanted to approach the publisher with something more than just a plea. Perhaps, he reasoned, Manchester could supply it to him. Kennedy knew that Thomas was to meet with the author the next morning and that shortly after, Manchester would sail for London. Goodwin and Marshall were dispatched to ambush him in the Berkshire, while the Senator himself stood in reserve a few blocks away. Sending Marshall seemed like a particularly happy thought. The relationship between Manchester and Goodwin was deteriorating, and nearly everyone liked Burke Marshall. (Evan Thomas, who is not very good at remembering names, always referred to Marshall as "the nice guy, what's his name?")

The gambit failed. As the author of *The Death of a President,* Manchester would have made a powerful ally against *Look.* Earlier, Mrs. Kennedy and Dick Goodwin had hoped he would actively campaign for changes in the manuscript, perhaps even *force Look* to sue him. By mid-November, however, it might have been enough if Manchester would just associate himself with the changes. When he would not, Kennedy was left to approach Cowles with only another plea.

When they met, Kennedy told Cowles that the revisions most urgently desired by Mrs. Kennedy lay in six areas of the serialization—two scenes by her husband's coffin, two in their bedroom, and the texts of the two letters she and Caroline had sent to the President. In these six areas, he said, there were only nine or ten changes that were truly important.

Goodwin had returned the proofs for the fourth and final installment of the serialization less than a month before, and Manchester and the *Look* editors, in fact, as they had in the first three installments, had incorporated some of the changes he had sought. In time, they made even more, but they felt put upon when they were *told* they had to make them.

For instance, the *Look* editors thought that Manchester had sprayed too much gore around the inside of the limousine in which Kennedy was shot and some of the descriptive passages were deleted. ("Too much hair and brains," Bill Attwood had decided. "Take them out.") They also thought that Manchester's account of how Maude Shaw told Caroline of her father's death was too sentimental. He had spread it over about six paragraphs. It was cut to one. ("Make it neater," Attwood said.)

Now, both these things—the gore, the conversation with Caroline—were things that Mrs. Kennedy wanted out. *Look* took them out, as it did other things, but it did not want to show the re-edited proofs to the Kennedys. *Look*'s lawyers told the editors not to, and *Look*'s editors agreed with the lawyers. They believed that if the Kennedys saw the changes that had been made, they would simply press on and ask for more.

Gardner Cowles therefore told Kennedy that he would not show the revised galley proofs to anyone outside the *Look* organization, but that Goodwin and Attwood could discuss them. Whereupon Goodwin and the editor-in-chief had a separate conference. Goodwin pressed Attwood to tell him precisely what changes had been made, and Attwood declined. Politely he told Goodwin that he was not "at liberty to do that," and that he could only discuss the general areas in which they had been made. It was another impasse.

On November 22, precisely three years after the assassination of John Kennedy, Mike Land of *Look* flew to London to get Manchester's approval on eight changes in the serialization. The changes, most of which originated in *Look*'s legal department, were inconsequential, changing the word "shooting" to "hunting," for instance, and they had been approved by Editor Bill Arthur and Managing Editor Bob Meskill. Some involved a word, some a sentence, and the longest was perhaps twenty words. Manchester agreed to all but one of the changes, and he was led to believe there would be no more, that the serialization would now stand intact. Land flew back the next day, wondering how he could justify such a brief trip to the accounting department.

A few days after Land met with Manchester, Cass Canfield and Evan Thomas met with Mrs. Kennedy. Canfield, the chairman of the executive committee of Harper & Row, had abstained from the flow of memoranda, the phone calls, and the consultations with Bob Kennedy, although he had, of course, guided a good many of them. His was a distinguished name in publishing. Cass Canfield, tall and erect, baldish, sixty-nine years old, out of Groton, Harvard, and Oxford, could move as easily in Hyannisport as he could in New York or Washington. Moreover, he had known Jacqueline Kennedy and been fond of her since his son had married her sister. When he met with her to discuss *The Death of a President* he said that he himself would visit Manchester in

London, and he suggested that he carry with him some word from her. She wrote:

NOVEMBER 28, 1966

DEAR BILL:

Cass Canfield and Evan Thomas are bringing you memoranda concerning the *Look* transcript and your book. They have asked me to write so that you will have no doubt about the changes made—that are asked for. I cannot see why any letter is necessary after all that has happened—with all the efforts we have made—and I have made personally to handle this in a way that is least painful to us all. But so there is no doubt—from all that has been told to me—the changes I am talking about—that Cass Canfield has with him—all touch upon things of a personal nature that I cannot bear to be made public. There are many other matters I know, but these are all of that sort, and are absolutely necessary to me and my children. I cannot believe that you will not do this much.

Sincerely,

JACQUELINE KENNEDY

The memoranda that Mrs. Kennedy spoke about had been drawn up by Dick Goodwin, and they listed twenty-five areas in the book and ten in the serialization to which she objected. After he got them, Canfield left Mrs. Kennedy's Fifth Avenue apartment and visited Gardner Cowles at *Look*, showing him the memoranda and telling him that he and Thomas would leave for London the next day to reason with Manchester. Cowles had not known of the trip, and he thought it odd that the head of Harper & Row should be showing him a memorandum from Mrs. Kennedy that dealt with something in *Look* magazine. He was not at all pleased.

On November 29, Canfield and Thomas flew to London, where they checked into Manchester's hotel, an elegant old establishment in Mayfair called the Connaught, and arranged to meet the author the next day in the office of his London agent, A. D. Peters, at 10 Buckingham Street. By then, Manchester was ailing. The slight cold he picked up in Middletown had turned into a raging fever, and in a day or so the fever would reach 104 degrees. Even when he had been at his best in those last few months he had been handicapped by the residue of more than two years' fatigue; the fever pulled him down further.

At Peters' office, Canfield gave him the letter from Mrs. Kennedy. He read it. Then he was handed the memoranda, and he read them. As Mrs. Kennedy had said, they dealt with passages of a personal nature. The memorandum about *Look,* for instance, showed that she objected to the following things in the serialization:

1—A conversation in which she spoke about Governor Connally.

2—A bedroom scene in Fort Worth.

3—A description of her at a dressing table, looking for lines in her face and musing about Dallas blondes.

4—References to blood, brains, and skull in the President's car.

5—Two passages about her thoughts and actions as she stood by the President's coffin.

6—Her instructions to Malcolm Kilduff, a White House press assistant, to tell the reporters aboard Air Force One that she did not want to sit with the Johnsons, that she would remain with the coffin.

7—A conversation with Secretary of Defense Robert S. McNamara in which she compared her love for her children with her love for her husband.

8—A description of her in bed at the White House on the night of the assassination.

9—Caroline's reaction on learning of the death of her father.

10—References to the letters she placed in the coffin.

Manchester looked at the list, and then he glanced at the page proofs Canfield had given him. They were marked with red ink and they had paper clips attached to each page on which there was a request for a change. The first page that he looked at was not about Mrs. Kennedy or her children. It did not touch on them. It told of Lyndon Johnson's first Cabinet meeting as President.

Peters, who is usually referred to as the dean of British literary agents, recalls that Manchester looked at the proofs with "astonishment," and then said angrily that he had to examine them before he could make a decision. That afternoon, Manchester spurned an invitation from Canfield and Thomas to sit with them at lunch. Glowering, he sat alone. Examining the proofs, he found requests for changes on twenty-nine of them. Later, at a meeting in his hotel room, he told Canfield and Thomas that he would make revisions on sixteen of the twenty-nine, but that he would make no more.

Underlining the point, Manchester recalls, he drew up a memo, this one two pages, on which he "summarized the events of the day." The primary point was that there would be no more requests for revisions in the book. Each of the four men—Manchester, Thomas, Canfield, and Peters—solemnly signed the memorandum and initialed the clauses in which there had been changes. Late that afternoon, when it was time for Canfield and Thomas to return to New York, they asked Manchester to ride with them out to the airport. He did, and the trip turned into an argument that continued until the editors reached Customs. Canfield and Thomas still thought Manchester should honor all of Mrs. Kennedy's requests. Manchester said no, the requests were political, not personal.

The argument ended when they learned that the plane for New York had been delayed by mechanical trouble in Munich. Canfield and Thomas decided to remain overnight in the hotel at London airport, while Peters and Manchester, who was nearly collapsed from fever and exhaustion, returned to the hotel.

While Canfield dozed, Thomas reviewed the proofs on which Manchester had been working. They were not right. Manchester had not made all the changes the editor had expected. (It seems to have been the old problem: What is a change? A word? A sentence? A great rewriting?) At about eleven that evening he called Manchester at the Connaught. Would he make the changes Mrs. Kennedy wanted? Manchester said he had done enough. But he must make them, Thomas told him. Manchester mentioned the memorandum they had signed that afternoon. He would not hear of further changes. Then, Thomas said, Harper & Row could not publish the book. Manchester, sweating into a fever of 104, hung up.

Neither man seems to have understood the other that night. Thomas, not without compassion, says that "it was all confused." Manchester recalls it as "bleak, very bleak." The author, "in a state of shock," called Don Congdon in New York and said he was turning everything over to him. Canfield, meanwhile, flew back to New York, telling Thomas to stay behind for a further attempt at getting Manchester to revise his manuscript. It was, of course, hopeless. Four days later, Manchester wrote to Congdon:

"I have reached the point where, if the integrity of my manuscript is violated, I have no wish to go on living. It sounds vainglorious, I know, but I am ready to die for this book."

Within hours of his arrival in New York, Canfield had called Mrs. Kennedy and told her it was important that he see her. A meeting was hastily convened the same day in

Simon Rifkind's office, and Canfield triumphantly told Mrs. Kennedy:

"I have applied the ultimate sanction that is in the power of the publisher to apply."

He meant he would not publish the book unless Manchester complied with her requests. Goodwin, who was also at the meeting, says sourly that "Canfield was the hero of the hour." The battle was ended. Manchester must make the changes, or be without a book. With a flourish, Canfield left the office, arm in arm with Mrs. Kennedy.

Thomas returned from London that same day and reported to Canfield that Manchester was still implacable. That evening both men went to Canfield's home, calling Congdon and presenting him with Harper & Row's ultimatum. Congdon, in turn, called across the Atlantic and told Manchester of the conversation. Meanwhile, Jackie Kennedy, who still had not read *The Death of a President,* was sitting in her apartment, deep in discussion with Rifkind, Burke Marshall, and Dick Goodwin. Harper & Row had capitulated. There was only *Look,* and it was decided that Mrs. Kennedy would make one last plea to Gardner Cowles.

The next morning, Canfield called Cowles and told him it was urgent that they meet. Cowles agreed, and they chose a time in the afternoon. At 1 P.M., just as Cowles was getting ready to go to lunch, a messenger appeared with a four-page, handwritten letter from Jackie Kennedy. It said she had talked too freely to Manchester, and that she had relied on his good taste and good faith, but that she had been deceived. Then she wrote: *"I have considered bringing a lawsuit to halt your printing of the book. However, to sue would only dramatize and increase the attention on the most offensive parts."*

That was Friday, December 2, and that afternoon, Cowles and Jack Harding met with Thomas and Canfield, who told

them of the trip to London. Harriet F. Pilpel, an attorney
with Greenbaum, Wolff & Ernst, the firm that represents
Harper & Row, was there part of the time, too—one of the
first of a staggering number of lawyers who got involved with
The Death of a President.

Mrs. Kennedy had once told Manchester that she thought
his book might be a slender little affair, bound in black, perhaps, and tucked away on library shelves as a footnote to
history. By December 2, however, the possibility that *The
Death of a President* would be anything but a major event in
publishing had been irretrievably lost. The Book-of-the-
Month Club had offered $250,000 as an advance against
royalties for the right to distribute it to its members. There
were estimates in the publishing world that ultimately it
could be a million-dollar deal. Furthermore, by December 2
Harper & Row had begun to revise its estimate of a first
printing of 40,000 copies, and it was thinking in terms of
100,000 copies. (Eventually it was to decide on a first printing of 600,000, perhaps the most extraordinary figure of all,
although it limited its profit to no more than 6 percent of
the net receipts on the first 100,000 copies. The rest it would
turn over to the Kennedy Library.)

By December 2, the manuscript for the book was at the
printers, and Harper & Row thought it could be published
in March. *Look,* which was paying $665,000 for the right to
serialize it, had already resold foreign rights to a number of
overseas publications, and it planned to put the first installment on the newsstands on January 10. *Look,* too, had its
manuscript at the printers, and the Cowles executives knew
that if a legal suit forced them to skip an issue it would cost
the company between three million and five million dollars.
Moreover, *Look* was certain that it had every right to publish
the serialization, and Gardner Cowles was reluctant to agree
with Cass Canfield that Bill Manchester must continue to

make changes in his manuscript. If Harper & Row did refuse to publish *The Death of a President, Look* would find itself serializing a phantom, a book that never was.

So peculiar pressures to publish were building up, and the pressures were only complicated by everyone knowing everyone else, by old ties of friendship and family, and by the fact that from the very beginning everyone just assumed that everything would, of course, turn out all right in the end. Furthermore, by December 2 some people in the dispute were mad at one another and this could hardly help things either. (For instance, there had been some serious discussion at *Look* about making all the changes the Kennedys wanted, and then publishing the serialization under a subtitle: "As Edited by the Kennedy Family." When Harding asked Robert Kennedy in November what he thought of the idea, the Senator had looked coldly at him and said: "I don't have to explain to you, Mr. Harding." Harding is a mild man, but months later when he recalled the exchange the tips of his ears still turned red.)

Possibly no one person knows what happened in those next few days after Canfield and Thomas returned from London, but something happened, and if it was no one thing then it was a series of the small things that had made *The Death of a President* an impossible project from the start. On December 5, Canfield, Thomas, Mrs. Pilpel, and Nancy Weschler, another attorney from Greenbaum, Wolff & Ernst, met and compared the *Look* galleys with the page proofs for the book. The next day they met with Gardner Cowles, Bill Attwood, and Managing Editor Bob Meskill, and the book and the serialization were edited so that they conformed. If you prefer to believe, as some columnists did, that the controversy over *The Death of a President* seriously impaired Robert Kennedy's chances of becoming President of the United States, then history was made that afternoon when

Cowles answered the letter that Jackie Kennedy had written to him a few days before. Both he *and* Canfield, he wrote, thought the book was in good taste and saw no need for further changes. "I realize you may not be entirely happy about all particulars," he said, "but I feel we have gone the limit to try to be fair and thoughtful of everyone's feelings— but yet consistent with accuracy."

The letter, Dick Goodwin insists, was the final indignity. Mrs. Kennedy had given up hope that *Look* would yield, but *Harper & Row!* On December 9, Robert Kennedy spoke to Canfield and Thomas. Immediately afterward he told Simon Rifkind that both had acknowledged that the manuscript had never been approved by himself or Mrs. Kennedy, but that they would publish on the basis of their agreement with Manchester. Rifkind, in turn, sent a warning to Cass Canfield that concluded:

> Unless we receive written confirmation from you by noon Monday, December 12, 1966, that you will not proceed with any publication of the Manchester manuscript in any form without hereafter securing approval of the manuscript by Mrs. Kennedy and the other approvals and consents which are required under the original Memorandum of Understanding referred to above and that you will submit the manuscript in the form for which you wish to have approval to us for examination by our client at the earliest possible date, we shall be compelled to take such action as we may deem appropriate to our client's rights.

He meant, of course, that Jackie might sue, and that same day Rifkind wrote to Gardner Cowles and told him that Mrs. Kennedy had not approved either Manchester's full manuscript or the part of it that *Look* might serialize. He said that "no action or failure to act by our client—and specifically no failure of our client to institute legal proceedings to enforce her rights by injunctive relief either prior to or after this date" would mean that Mrs. Kennedy had approved the manuscript. Rifkind did not, however, say that Mrs. Kennedy might sue, and the *Look* executives were a little puzzled. No one could really believe that she would, and they wondered what would happen next.

What happened next is that Jacqueline Kennedy told Simon Rifkind to sue. She did not care what kinds of papers he filed, she said, just so he filed something.

Nine

———————⟋⟍⟍⟋⟍⟍⟍⟍⟍⟍⟍⟍⟍⟍———————

I
T HAD never been a close secret that Mrs. Kennedy was unhappy about *The Death of a President*. In October, *Books*,
an enterprising literary monthly, reported that she wanted
Harper & Row to cancel publication, and the world of books
and authors and publishers had been rolling with rumors
ever since. Homer Bigart of *The Times* had discovered in
August that *something* was up, and that same month a news-
magazine posted a reporter near Manchester's vacation retreat in Maine to see if he could find out what was happening.
(He could not.) However, it was not until December 10, a
Saturday, that the big publications truly got onto the story.
On that day the Chicago *Daily News* said that Mrs. Kennedy
was dismayed about the book and that she regretted having
confided in Manchester, but that she had decided not to sue.
The Chicago *Daily News* was wrong, which was not surprising, since no one, including Robert Kennedy, had expected
her to sue.

Nonetheless, throughout that weekend calls went out from
reporters to the men who knew Robert Kennedy. Burke
Marshall, Professor Richard Neustadt of Harvard, Daniel P.

Moynihan of the Center for Advanced Studies at Wesleyan, who was an Assistant Secretary of Labor in the Kennedy Administration, and William vanden Heuvel, a sometime public servant and sometime politician from New York, all delivered themselves of emphatic "no comments." Dick Goodwin said that Mrs. Kennedy would have to speak for herself, but he allowed that she did have some reservations about the book several months ago, "probably about a few personal things, not terribly extensive. Since the whole is still in a state of change," he said, "the reservations may now be satisfied."

Ed Guthman, himself a Pulitzer Prize winner as a newspaperman, was more expansive. For the record, he would confirm only that he had read the manuscript for Senator Kennedy and that he had made some suggestions about it to Harper & Row. Off the record, for the time being, he said that "history is never monkeyed around with in the book" and that any hostility between the Kennedys and Lyndon Johnson was explained well and "with compassion." A problem, he said, was that Manchester apparently had lost control of the material that was to appear in *Look*. For instance, he said, there was "a lot of tension" aboard Air Force One on the flight from Dallas to Washington and that the use of excerpts from the book might make it "pretty tough" for the reader to "judge" the people on the plane. There could be a lack of perspective, he said, and the passengers could look less "sympathetic" than if they were seen in the context of the full book. Guthman, however, was reluctant to say anything at all about Mrs. Kennedy's objections, only that they dealt with "little things, interesting historical things, what she wore and said and did after the assassination, but not things vital to the book." All in all, it was probably as good a summation of the book as was to appear during the dispute from any partisan.

Unaccountably, Gardner Cowles said that he knew of no
pressure from the Kennedys to block publication of either
the book or the serialization. Evan Thomas tried to be cir-
cumspect, but then admitted that the publication of *The
Death of a President* was being delayed from March until
April while the author made a few changes in the manuscript.
Moreover, when he was asked if the Kennedys had sought
the changes because of Mrs. Kennedy's feelings, he said quite
unexpectedly:

"It is impossible to say as to their motives."

Neither Cowles nor Thomas nor Manchester, who was
then on the *Queen Mary,* knew what to expect that weekend.
They did not know much more, in fact, when they received
summonses from Mrs. Kennedy in the next two days. Simon
Rifkind, at Mrs. Kennedy's behest, had drawn them hastily,
and they showed only that she would pursue court action.
Harper & Row was served late Monday afternoon, and *Look*
early Tuesday morning, which was the same day Manchester
debarked, alone and weary, from the *Queen Mary.*

"If they give me a big prize rolled in gold and polished to
blind the cosmos, I'll just say 'Thanks,'" Manchester once
wrote to Jackie Kennedy, and now, a few months later, he
went to the *Look* offices, was told that the magazine had been
served not with a prize but a summons, and stayed there to
await his. When none came he left for a friend's home in
Connecticut, pursued by private detectives in cars, who surrounded the home, demanded that he appear, and then served
the summons.

That was Tuesday, and on Wednesday, when it was all
very big news, Robert Kennedy's colleagues mobilized themselves. Everything had happened suddenly, and they were uncomfortable, and so was Robert Kennedy. Jackie had given
him a great and overwhelming problem. In the next few
weeks many thousands, probably millions, of words were

written about the battle, and the words, which spread around the world, were inspired, most of them, not by Bobby, not by Lyndon, not even by the book itself, but by Jackie, who, while all these words were being written, managed to remain almost supernaturally aloof.

Possibly as much nonsense has been written about Jackie Kennedy as anyone else in America. She is one of America's great commodities, and she sells newspapers and magazines and books. Robert Kennedy does, too, and they both know it, and like most people, they would prefer that only nice things be written about them. Indeed, there is a convention that goes with most things that are written about Jackie Kennedy: It is acceptable to say nearly anything if the story somewhere, somehow, declares or implies love, respect, and honest concern for her well-being. At the height of the Manchester affair, when *The Daily News,* along with most of the other 1,700 or so daily newspapers in the country, was hustling for pieces and scraps of what was *really* in *The Death of a President,* it carried an extraordinary story with a great banner headline that said Jackie was still America's queen, a peacherino, and a national asset. *The Daily News* had small use for John Kennedy and probably less for Robert, but this was incidental. *The Daily News* would sooner have knocked the Washington Monument than Jackie Kennedy.

Lots of people, however, will knock Bobby, and explore Bobby, and try to plumb Bobby's depths, and it does not much matter to them whether they say good things about him or not. The Senator had authorized William Manchester to write a book. He had been involved in its creation only peripherally, and then in an enormous miscalculation he had offhandedly tried to suppress it. When that failed he had his people try to edit it, and when that didn't quite work out either he wanted to forget it. Instead he found himself involved in a great doughy dispute in which no one was truly right and no one was truly wrong, and there were no winners, only losers.

Columnists who shill regularly or periodically for the Kennedys wrote that the Senator leaped instinctively to join Mrs. Kennedy in the dispute, and that it was all a matter of family, this sprawling Irish family that apparently had come over from County Wexford the week before last and was now withdrawing into itself, while Robert, his bog trotter's blood at a boil, jumped in flailing to defend his sister-in-law. Family ties may be of supreme importance to the Kennedys, but the Senator is not ingenuous and he is not without means. He has, in fact, a formidable apparatus and it worked so effectively that the Senator seldom had to appear to say a word in either his own or Mrs. Kennedy's behalf and Mrs. Kennedy had to appear not at all. For instance, on Wednesday Mrs. Kennedy issued a statement through her office. The statement was written by Ted Sorensen, John Kennedy's old assistant and speech writer, and it said:

> Look Magazine, Harper & Row and Mr. William Manchester have repeatedly made clear that only legal action can alter their insistence upon publishing at this time—without regard to accepted standards of propriety and good faith, and in specific violation of my wishes, my contract with Mr. Manchester, and the dignity and privacy my children and I have striven with difficulty to retain—a premature account of the events of November, 1963, that is in part both tasteless and distorted.
>
> Its inaccurate and unfair references to other individuals, in contrast with its generous references to all members of the Kennedy family, are perhaps beyond my prevention; but to expose to all the world at this time all the private grief, personal thoughts and painful reactions my children and I endured in those terrible days does not seem to me to be essential to any current historical record.
>
> I am shocked that Mr. Manchester would exploit the emo-

tional state in which I recounted my recollections to him early in 1964, and I'm equally shocked that reputable publishers would take commercial advantage of his failure to keep his word. To the author and publishers this book will only be another transient chapter in their works, but my children and I will have to live with it for the rest of our lives.

As horrible as a trial will be, it now seems clear that my only redress is to ask the courts to enforce my rights and postpone publication until the minimum limits of my family's privacy can be protected.

That afternoon, a background briefing for the press was held in Mrs. Kennedy's office on Park Avenue. Perhaps a dozen reporters, television commentators, and columnists were invited, and the ground rules stipulated that they could not identify anyone who took part in the briefing by name and they could not attribute any remarks to them. This is an honorable and equitable method of dealing with the press and it is used throughout the Government. It probably had never been used before, however, to deal with a book, and it gave birth to the first of an enormous number of stories that were attributed to "a spokesman for Mrs. Kennedy," "a friend of the Kennedys," "a colleague of the Senator's," or simply "sources."

Burke Marshall was the spokesman that day, and he was assisted by Dick Goodwin and John Seigenthaler. Frank Mankiewicz, the Senator's press secretary, stood nearby chain-smoking Kools, while Pamela Turnure, perfectly free of makeup and buttoned up in a cardigan, leaned against a file cabinet. Everyone else in the small stuffy room, which ordinarily was used to store stationery, was wedged around a long wooden table.

That morning there had appeared a story in *The New York Times* saying that publication of *The Death of a President* could embarrass Senator Kennedy and damage the relationship between him and President Johnson. It was true, and Kennedy and his advisers had worried about it. Moreover, in the last few months at least some of the advisers, if not the Senator himself, had speculated about Kennedy's chances of winning the Vice-Presidential nomination from Hubert Humphrey in 1968, thus virtually assuring himself of the Presidential nomination in 1972. But if this were to be a reality there could hardly be discordance, or even the appearance of discordance, between Robert Kennedy and Lyndon Johnson. It was, therefore, important that the controversy over *The Death of a President* be presented in apolitical terms, as a story of a widow who had been wronged.

"I think Mrs. Kennedy's statement speaks for itself," Marshall said. "The reason that Mrs. Kennedy has filed this lawsuit is because this book contains material that was taken from private interviews that she gave under circumstances that were very painful, and she no doubt thought she would be protected from what is about to happen."

"What is the objectionable material?"

"It is personal and private. There isn't anything that is wrong in any other sense."

"Why did she file suit?"

"Parts would be too personal for anyone else except Mrs. Kennedy and the family."

The questions were polite; the atmosphere of the room was intimate; the spokesmen were respected. None of the reporters really knew what the hell the thing was about anyway, and none was prepared to tax Marshall, Goodwin, or Seigenthaler with hard questions about the effect of the book or the suit on the Senator's career. Still, they felt bound by duty to at least move in that direction, and after a long colloquy on the chronology of Manchester's book and how it was written, a man asked timidly:

"But, Burke, what is the reason for the suit?"

"It involves breach of faith on matters that are personal," Marshall said, with only a small trace of annoyance. After all, he had been asked that question before.

"Is there anything in the book that reflects unfavorably on any member of the Kennedy family?"

"No."

(That was close. The reporter could have asked if the book reflected unfavorably on any assistant to a member of the Kennedy family.)

"Is there anything in the book that would be harmful to the Senator's political career?"

There it was, right out in the open, and Marshall said slowly and positively:

"No, there is nothing harmful to the Senator's political career."

Burke Marshall does not lie. Of course, he had not read the book, but neither had Ted Sorensen, who wrote the statement calling it "tasteless and distorted." Nonetheless, Marshall was contradicting some of the Senator's advisers who had read the book and then decided that it could harm the Senator's career. None of them had publicly announced this, but they had discussed it and worried about it and tried to edit out what they thought was most damaging. When *The Death of a President* was published it was a little difficult to see what, exactly, everyone had been so worried about, and in fact the most damaging thing to the Senator was not the book but the argument itself. After the suit had been resolved, a poll by Lou Harris showed that 69 percent of the public had followed the controversy surrounding *The Death of a President,* and that 20 percent of the public "thought less" of the Senator because of it. Moreover, among those citizens who said they had followed the controversy closely there was a sharp shift in their choice for the 1968 Presidential nomination. They preferred Lyndon Johnson to Robert

Kennedy by 59 to 41 percent, while people who did not follow the controversy wanted Kennedy rather than Johnson, 54 to 46 percent.

Polls come and go, the public is fickle, and in time the battle of the book will be musty. But when Burke Marshall was holding the briefing the battle was very hot, and Marshall gave not the slightest indication that there was any political consideration involved. He spoke only of Mrs. Kennedy's suit, of her personal feelings, and of her need for privacy. He did not specify what, precisely, she objected to in the book, and none of the reporters asked him. He did not mention President Johnson by name either, although he implied he was treated fairly in the book, and soon the reporters were prefacing questions with statements like, "Now, Burke, there's nothing critical of President Johnson in the book," while Burke would answer the question squarely in terms of Mrs. Kennedy's feelings.

It was a splendid performance, made more so by the fact that most reporters empathize with the Kennedys and their colleagues and are charmed by them. The Kennedys and their colleagues are, in fact, good company. Moreover, they are liberals, and so are most reporters. They are also powerful men who have been places and done things, and they offer reporters the promise of excitement, of being close to the things that matter, of being nearly a participant in events and not just an observer. The Senator himself has honored friendly writers by dropping in on their parties, and there are competent reporters who treasure their PT-109 tie clips. These things in themselves are not wicked, but they tend to give the Kennedys an advantage over most politicians. Probably a reporter ought not to like any of his news sources; certainly he ought to hold them at arm's length, but it is a difficult thing to do when they are spokesmen for the Kennedys, and sometimes there is a mad desire to please them.

In the next few weeks, the suit over *The Death of a President* was resolved in the *Look* offices, in hastily summoned conferences at lawyers' suites, in the board room at Harper & Row, in the Berkshire Hotel, over luncheon in a private club just off Fifth Avenue, and in Jackie Kennedy's apartment. The real battle, however, was fought in newspapers and magazines, and it might have been fought exactly along the lines that Burke Marshall had laid down in that first briefing, a simple case of breach of contract, if the plaintiff in the case had been anyone other than Jackie Kennedy.

A few hours after she issued her statement, *Look* and Harper & Row put out statements. They were calm recitals of the chronology of the dispute and they did not, of course, touch on all the nuances of the publishers' cases because the publishers' cases were far too complex. A few hours after they were released it was difficult to remember what they said, while Mrs. Kennedy's statement ("tasteless and distorted," "inaccurate and unfair references to other individuals," "I am shocked that Mr. Manchester would exploit the emotional state in which I recounted my recollections," "as horrible as a trial will be") lent itself nicely to newspaper stories and to speculation about Jackie herself.

Since the assassination, the responsible press had laid off Mrs. Kennedy. There had been innumerable little stories about what her office always referred to as her "holidays," and they always began, "Mrs. John F. Kennedy left here yesterday for a three-week holiday in Hawaii," or the West Indies, or Sun Valley, and they were always followed by stories that began, "Mrs. John F. Kennedy returned here yesterday from a three-week holiday in Hawaii," or the West Indies, or Sun Valley. The suit to suppress *The Death of a President*, however, legitimatized another kind of story. Everyone wanted to know what it was that Mrs. Kennedy was objecting to, and the suit touched off a mad competition among reporters to find out. Many of the details in the manuscript that Mrs. Kennedy found offensive received an airing in the press, and everything that she presumably hoped to prevent with a suit happened anyway. There was some solemn talk about the public's right to know these things, as well as some sanctimonious chanting from columnists and magazine writers who insisted that other publications, never their own, were being indecent in exposing Mrs. Kennedy's secrets and private griefs. Still, it was inevitable that they would be exposed, and that Mrs. Kennedy would be wounded. America has made Mrs. Kennedy its public property.

Other people and things were wounded in the press, too. One of them was William Manchester, and another was *The Death of a President. Time* magazine, four months before the book was published, confidently reported that it "paints, in fact, an almost unrelieved portrait of Johnson as an unfeeling and boorish man." *Time,* as did nearly every other publication, said the book also told of Kenny O'Donnell, John Kennedy's old friend and assistant, literally blocking Lyndon Johnson's way when he attempted to disembark from Air Force One with Mrs. Kennedy aboard the fork lift that was rolled up to the plane's door in Washington. The fork-lift incident does not appear in the book, and the book certainly did not paint "an almost unrelieved portrait of Johnson as an unfeeling and boorish man." Moreover, *Time* reported that Manchester's book was "seriously flawed by the fact that its partisan portrayal of Lyndon Johnson is so hostile that it almost demeans the office itself."

When the book was published, however, the two-page review in *Time* said: "During the height of his battle with the Kennedys, it was said that Manchester had depicted Lyndon Johnson as a kind of Snopesian boor in the hours immediately after the assassination. L.B.J.'s portrait as it now appears in the book is not all that uncomplimentary." Indeed it was not; it never was. *Time* had been getting its information from the wrong people.

Meanwhile, other voices than the Kennedys' were spreading the word about *The Death of a President*. For instance, Bennett Cerf, the chairman of the board of Random House, speaking informally at a dinner at Yale University, said he had read the unedited manuscript of Manchester's book and that it told of "the unbelievable things that happened after the assassination. *The Death of a President,*" he said, "will sell a million copies if it is allowed to be published, and although the Kennedys are kicking I think it will be."

Cerf was being prescient, and early the next afternoon Martin Gold, a member of Simon Rifkind's firm, walked into the County Courthouse in downtown Manhattan and filed Mrs. Kennedy's suit with Saul S. Streit, the ranking justice of the State Supreme Court. Rifkind had prepared the papers in the suit with the aid of Edward Costikyan, another lawyer in his firm, who was once the head of the regular Democratic organization in Manhattan, and they were far more extensive than had been expected. There was a copy of the original Memorandum of Understanding, some correspondence, copies of *Look* advertisements in which Mrs. Kennedy's name was mentioned prominently, a fifteen-page complaint and an eleven-page affidavit by Mrs. Kennedy, and, perhaps most important, a five-page affidavit in support of the suit from Senator Kennedy. He said: "I categorically state that at no time did I ever give my approval or consent to the text of the manuscript, to any publication thereof, or to any time of publication; nor did I ever say or do anything from which the defendants could reasonably have believed that I did. To my knowledge, neither did plaintiff."

That was the heart of the matter, and after speaking of

the telegram in which he had said that "members of the Kennedy family will place no obstacle in the way of publication" of *The Death of a President,* the Senator dealt with the intermediaries who had represented both himself and Mrs. Kennedy in editing the book, selling the magazine rights, and working with Manchester. He said:

> Defendants may assert that, because certain of Mrs. Kennedy's friends read portions of the manuscript and made suggestions as to its text, Mrs. Kennedy and I have somehow approved the manuscript. But the fact is that no one who read the manuscript had authority to approve it on behalf of Mrs. Kennedy or me. Nor did I have authority from Mrs. Kennedy to approve it on her behalf. I never asserted such authority. I am informed and believe that no one asserted that he had such authority to speak for me or Mrs. Kennedy, and there is no basis for any of the defendants to believe that anyone other than plaintiff and I were in a position to approve for each of us respectively.
>
> Neither I nor Mrs. Kennedy has ever seen the text as written by defendant Manchester. Moreover, neither of us has any knowledge of how much, if at all, the proposed text of the book or of the magazine serialization varies from the material originally written by defendant Manchester. We cannot be said to have approved what we have never seen.

In her affidavit, Mrs. Kennedy reviewed the history of the book and said that *Look* was inducing Manchester to break his contract with Robert Kennedy. Of Harper & Row she said:

> Until very recently, Harper took the position that it would not publish the manuscript until I had given my approval, both as to the mode and time of publication and the text of the manuscript. Very recently, however, Harper has changed its position and has indicated that it intends to go ahead with publication in March or April of 1967.

And as for the approval, Mrs. Kennedy said:

> I have never seen Manchester's manuscript. I have not approved it, nor have I authorized anyone else to approve it for me.
>
> I cannot be said to have approved what I have never seen, and yet, because it is widely known that I personally (and the Kennedy family) extended so much help to defendant Manchester, it will only be natural for the public to believe that the manuscript is published with my approval.

In her complaint, Mrs. Kennedy asked the court for five forms of relief. First, she asked that Harper & Row, *Look*, and Manchester be prevented from publishing the manuscript and from allowing others to publish it until she had approved both the text and the date of publication. She also asked that they be prevented from giving anyone a copy of the manuscript without her approval. Second, she asked that the defendants be permanently barred from publishing or using letters from herself and from Caroline to the President, and she asked that any letters or copies of letters in Manchester's possession be returned to her. Her third request was that the defendants be forbidden from using the tape recordings of her conversations with Manchester and that the tapes and all copies be returned to her. Fourth, she asked that Cowles Communications be permanently enjoined from using her name in its advertisements, which, she said, had violated her rights under Sections 50 and 51 of the New York State Civil Rights Act. The sections protect the right of privacy and say that the use, without written consent, of anyone's name, portrait, or picture for advertising is a misdemeanor. Finally, Mrs. Kennedy said, she wanted the court to embody all her rights in a declaration and to award her both compensatory and punitive damages, as well as the cost of the suit. "The threatened publication," she said, "is in total disregard of my rights and, if it goes forward, will utterly destroy them."

Justice Streit said he would hold a hearing on the case December 27, eleven days from then, and that he would issue a verdict shortly thereafter. *Look,* however, planned to put the first installment on the newsstands January 10 in the issue that had a cover date of January 24, and the printers, R. R. Donnelly & Sons of Chicago, had already started to work on it. "We are going right ahead with a normal schedule," Editor Bill Arthur said with more confidence than he felt. Generally, magazines need at least twenty days before distribution to print a four-color section, and Mrs. Kennedy, as Bill Attwood said later, had *Look* hung up on the presses. Moreover, *Look* had another problem. If it waited until December 27 for the hearing, and then waited a few days more for Justice Streit's decision, it would lose its issue even if it won the suit. The executives at *Look* estimated that this would cost the magazine from three million to five million dollars, plus an unimaginable toll in production and distribution problems.

Consequently, it behooved *Look* and everyone else for that matter to reach an agreement with Mrs. Kennedy. Although from the outside it appeared that positions were rigid and that only Justice Streit could untangle things with a court decree, there had been a good deal of conversation among the participants in the dispute. In fact, Justice Streit could have chosen an earlier date than December 27 for a hearing, but the attorneys for all sides, even before the suit was filed, had told him there was at least a possibility that things could be settled out of court. Justice Streit was giving them time.

Now Mrs. Kennedy contended that neither *Look* nor Harper & Row had allowed her to see the final proofs of the material it would use, while *Look* and Harper & Row said

THE MANCHESTER AFFAIR   184

that she had never asked to see them for herself, only for her representatives. On the day the suit was filed, *Look* agreed to show Mrs. Kennedy the proofs at what was to be a secret meeting the next day at the office of its attorney, David W. Peck, a former presiding justice of the Appellate Division of the State Supreme Court, and, like Simon Rifkind, a man of parts. Peck had been as involved in Republican as Rifkind had been in Democratic politics, and his name had even been put forth from time to time as a candidate for office. He had also been a president of the State Bar Association, the chairman of a commission to revise the state constitution, and a mediator in a number of difficult labor disputes. He was above reproach, and so was his law firm, Sullivan & Cromwell, for whom he handled only important cases. (In 1965, for example, he had represented Notre Dame in its suit to ban the movie *John Goldfarb, Please Come Home*. It fantasized about the Notre Dame football team disporting itself with houris in a Middle Eastern harem, and Peck had asked the court: "Will we now have films showing Bryn Mawr brothels and Dartmouth dope dens?")

It was arranged that Mrs. Kennedy, accompanied by Rifkind and Goodwin, would stop in at Peck's office at 48 Wall Street at one o'clock Saturday afternoon. Wall Street would be deserted then, and since only the participants in the dispute knew about the meeting it would be private and off the record. Few things in the battle of the book, however, were ever private. There was a leak, of course—Manchester, who had been told of the meeting, mentioned it to a friend, who told a friend—and when Mrs. Kennedy's dark blue Oldsmobile turned down Wall Street a reporter and a photographer awaited her. Goodwin, recognizing the reporter, ordered the driver around the block to look for another entrance. There was none, and so there was a quick conversation in the Oldsmobile. Should the meeting go on as planned? Mrs. Kennedy said yes, and a few minutes later the Oldsmobile drew up outside 48 Wall Street.

Goodwin got out first. He looked mad. Mrs. Kennedy got out next. She looked dispassionate. Rifkind followed. He looked dignified. The conventional wisdom is that reporters badger Mrs. Kennedy. They do not. Mostly they hang about and shuffle their feet, and that afternoon Mrs. Kennedy, arm in arm with Rifkind, followed Goodwin past the reporter and photographer, who were standing in the doorway of 52, not 48, Wall Street, and into the wrong building. A janitor with a mop stared walleyed at Mrs. Kennedy, and a few moments later Judge Rifkind walked out, glanced at the numbers atop the doorways, went inside again, and emerged with Mrs. Kennedy. This time Goodwin followed them.

For the next two hours, Mrs. Kennedy sat with Goodwin and Bill Attwood and read the proofs of *The Death of a President*. She was composed and she did not cry, and she was, in fact, absorbed. Furthermore, she knew what it was that she wanted out of the serialization, and when she left she said to Attwood:

"You and Dick have a lot of work to do, so I'll leave you my cigarettes."

Then Mrs. Kennedy left, escorted by Rifkind, who had been conferring with Peck, Gardner Cowles, and Jack Harding in another room. Coming down in the elevator she remembered the newspapermen outside, and she tried to leave by a back exit. Finding it blocked, she and Rifkind went out the way they had come in, and when Mrs. Kennedy reappeared on Wall Street she was crying. She climbed into the Oldsmobile and was driven away. Rifkind stayed behind to answer questions.

What had they been doing?

"One of the problems has been that we did not have access to the text of the material. Judge Peck has made available to us the opportunity to look at it. I asked Mrs. Kennedy to come along in case she had any comment to make on any of the material which we observed in the text."

Had Mrs. Kennedy read it?

"She has not seen the material, but when we asked her a question with respect to an event or something of that kind she was available so that she could respond to such questions."

Was she upset?

"She was upset. Partly she was upset because this was supposed to be an opportunity to inspect unaccompanied by a high order of visibility. This meeting was arranged very quickly and with the understanding that this was not a settlement discussion, that this was just an opportunity to inspect. We said we wanted no publicity about it. Consequently we were somewhat distressed to find that the press was here."

That evening, a reporter called Rifkind and asked him again if Mrs. Kennedy had read the serialization. Again he said no, and then he qualified it, "at least not in my presence."

Still, the fact was that Mrs. Kennedy had read it, and she had been composed, and it made the *Look* editors hopeful. The next day, however, they read that she had left the meeting in tears. It began to seem ominous again. Why was she crying? Had someone said something wrong? In truth, they may have been a little afraid of Jackie. During the Kennedy Administration, *Look* once wanted to take pictures of John Kennedy, Jr. The President thought this would be fine, but Mrs. Kennedy, who felt the boy was too young to face a photographer, did not. Consequently, it was arranged that a photographer and writer would visit Hyannisport just after Mrs. Kennedy had gone on a vacation, leaving the children behind. The men from *Look* showed up at the appointed time and were strolling across the compound lawn when unaccountably they saw Mrs. Kennedy walking in their direction. They considered her far too formidable to face, and they scrambled under the porch of Joe Kennedy's home, waiting out the time in isolation until she had left and they could take their pictures.

The day after Mrs. Kennedy's visit to Peck's office, Bill Attwood met Dick Goodwin in the Senator's apartment to discuss the objections Mrs. Kennedy had just raised to the serialization. Robert Kennedy was not there. The night before he and his family and some friends had flown to Sun Valley, Idaho, for a Christmas skiing vacation. The Senator, in fact, had made only one public appearance since the Manchester dispute had broken forth, and that had been on the day Mrs. Kennedy filed suit. He had shown up at the Overseas Press Club in New York to associate himself with a committee to save St. Francis Hospital, a Catholic institution that the New York Archdiocese wanted to close, and he had attracted a phenomenal number of newspaper, television, and radio reporters, few of whom were much interested in St. Francis, but nearly all of whom wanted Kennedy to say something about *The Death of a President*. He did not. He slipped away and into an elevator without a word.

His New York apartment is not so much a home as an office. The real center of his life is in McLean, Virginia, of course, and the apartment is a sort of way station where meetings are held, friends are put up for the night, and Bobby changes his shirt. Only the wealthy live in the building, which has enormously discreet doormen, uniformed guards, and a great amount of carpeting. Kennedy's apartment itself has art on the walls, pictures of the family scattered about, and a curiously unlived-in atmosphere, like a suite for wealthy transients, which is really what it is. However, it is private, and Goodwin and Attwood worked there to revise the serialization. No matter what Mrs. Kennedy may have felt about the political revelations in *The Death of a President* she was not complaining about them. She was asking only that the personal passages be excised. The problem, however, was that she wanted them torn out in their entirety, rather than edited. *Look* was aghast at the idea, and Goodwin had prevailed on her to accept the idea of judicious editing. Mrs. Kennedy thought, for instance, that Manchester had written at unconscionable length about the reaction of Caroline Kennedy on learning of her father's death. Attwood and Goodwin reduced this to a single sentence: "The little girl buried her face in the pillow, crying." They went on, laboring until dark.

Manchester, meanwhile, was in Middletown, in effect, hiding out. His home had been surrounded by television cameramen when the dispute had become public knowledge, and for a while he had sought refuge with a friend. Although his phone was listed not in his name but in his wife's, by the end of the week enough newsmen had discovered the number so that it rang constantly. Mrs. Manchester, who accepted the calls, was a heavy smoker, anyway, but the strain was driving her up to four packs of Kools a day. Once, in the small hours of the morning on the day after Mrs. Kennedy had called her husband's book "tasteless and distorted," a Middletown policeman had pounded on her back door to tell her excitedly that people were saying bad things about her husband and that a reporter from New York had called the police department to enlist its aid in reaching him. The reporter, he said, wanted "to help" Manchester. It was a writer from an afternoon paper who was striving mightily to write a follow-up story to Mrs. Kennedy's attack, but who did not know Manchester's phone number. (There is a William Manchester listed in the Middletown phone book. It is, however, not the right one. No one knows how many times *his* phone rang that week.) Julia Manchester, who has a genuine passion about wasting public funds, sent the policeman away after telling him that he ought to be earning his salary in better ways.

Nonetheless, Manchester, who had great faith in the written word, wanted to make a statement. His attorney, Carleton G. Eldridge, Jr., of Coudert Brothers, one of the giants in the field of literary law, was reluctant to see his client in any kind of public debate with the Kennedys, but the author was persistent. Moreover, he was taking a beating. While Attwood and Goodwin were working on the proofs in New York, Senator Edward M. Kennedy was issuing his first statement in the dispute. From Washington he said that Manchester "now intends to go ahead in violation of the word of his agreement, the spirit of his agreement and despite the pain he knows it will give Mrs. Kennedy." He went on to say that "what is at stake is not his integrity as a writer nor the accuracy of history, but rather the integrity of the commitment and the promise he willingly and voluntarily made."

Meanwhile, there were reports from Austin, Texas, that some associates of President Johnson knew all about *The Death of a President* and were prepared to prove that it was all wrong. The President himself was staying out of it. James Reston of *The New York Times* had reported on Saturday that Bill D. Moyers, Johnson's press secretary, had read the "offending passages" and had undoubtedly informed the President of them. However, on Sunday, while Ted Kennedy was making his statement, Moyers said that he had not read the book and he had not "read anything to the President." Still, when he was asked if he was denying that he had read excerpts from *The Death of a President,* Moyers had said: "No, I'm not denying that and I'm not confirming it either. This is a tragic enough case already without the White House getting involved in it." Nonetheless, even if the White House did not want to get involved, men of God did. That morning, in a sermon at the Community Church in New York, the Reverend Dr. Donald S. Harrington, who had not read it, recommended that no one buy *The Death of a President* if it was published over Mrs. Kennedy's objections. Dr. Harrington, who had been the unsuccessful candidate for Lieutenant Governor the previous November on the Liberal Party ticket, said the matter was "simply a defense of right of privacy."

Manchester, of course, thought it was much more and he was eager to tell the world. He had drafted a statement a few days before, but the people at *Look* and Harper & Row considered it a little too impassioned. What was needed, they said, was restraint. Moreover, Manchester was in the throes of flu once more, and so his statement was filtered through Dick Collins, the *Look* public relations man. Collins, working it out as he lay sleepless on Saturday night, pared Manchester's words and worked in a little of the history of the dispute, but the heart of the statement was Manchester's, and *Look* released it on Sunday. "John Kennedy was my President," the author declared. "To suggest that I would dishonor his memory or my association with him is both cruel and unjust." In all he said:

> On July 29, 1966, I was informed by a member of the Kennedy family that because of President Kennedy's "respect" for me as "a historian and a reporter ... members of the Kennedy family will place no obstacle in the way of publication" of my work.
>
> I believe that I am now—in December of 1966—the same historian and reporter that I was in July and the same historian and reporter that I was in 1962 when President Kennedy expressed his confidence in me.
>
> I feel that I am the same, yet clearly circumstances are not. A legal obstacle is sought to be placed in the way of publication of my book, *The Death of a President*.
>
> I had hoped my book would be allowed to speak for itself, and I would not have to speak for it. This is no longer pos-

...ed atmosphere Gardner Cowles was prepared to ...herwise.

...al action all this time was taking place in the meet-...ween Attwood and Goodwin, who were delicately ...the 60,000-word serialization. Much of what was ...ng elsewhere was froufrou, and some of the things ...peared in the newspapers were not even that. When ...ard of Directors of Cowles Communications met for ...ual Christmas luncheon it was solemnly reported as ...-long meeting of top *Look* executives," huddling on a ...atic development." A little later a reporter called *Look* ...se he had discovered that "Melvin C. Wetmore" left ...rty precipitously. Did it mean there was a settlement? ...ally, Marvin C. Whatmore, the president of *Look*, left ...party because he had another engagement.

...Meanwhile, Attwood and Goodwin were making every ...empt to keep their work a secret, and despite the best ...orts of the nosy Parkers they were succeeding. (On Mon-...ay, the New Frontiersmen who were operating out of the ...partment even had the unlisted numbers on the Senator's ...white phones changed. Partly, however, this was just to get ...some sleep; reporters were forever calling in the middle of ...the night.) Attwood says that he and Goodwin excised only ...trivia, "a little gingerbread," from the serialization. "We left a good deal in," he says, "that could have been dispensed with."

In none of these things was Harper & Row deeply involved. *Look*'s deadline was more immediate, and it behooved all sides to settle this serialization first. For one thing, if the dispute wore on until December 27, when it was scheduled to reach court, *Look*'s printing and distribution problems could be so complicated that it could very well lose the issue, even if it won the suit. Besides, *Look* had already sold the foreign serialization rights to a number of overseas publica-

sible. The integrity of my book and my own honesty as a writer and a person have been attacked.

In life John Kennedy belonged to all Americans. His cruel murder deprived us all. I cannot help but feel that some of the present bitterness comes from the dark night-mare of his death and the impotence in the face of death which we felt then and feel now.

John Kennedy was my President. To suggest that I would dishonor his memory or my association with him is both cruel and unjust. His standards of excellence have guided me throughout this work. I believe John Kennedy, who was himself an historian, would have wanted his countrymen to know the truth of those terrible days, and I have dedi-cated myself for nearly three years to reliving and recon-structing them so that the truth could be faithfully and accurately recorded.

It has been said that my work is being published pre-maturely and that magazine serialization was not contem-plated by the Kennedy family. This is not so. In the summer of 1966, authorization was given by the family for publica-tion of the book in early 1967, to be preceded by serialization in *Look* magazine.

It has been said that I have broken faith with Mrs. Ken-nedy, that I took advantage of her confidence in me and that I recorded too faithfully her words and emotions. I do not believe this to be so.

Mrs. Kennedy asked me to write this book; I did not seek the opportunity. Mrs. Kennedy gave me 10 hours of inter-views; I did not, indeed could not, have conducted these interviews without her voluntary cooperation. Mrs. Kennedy herself did not ask to see the manuscript and still hasn't. If she had, I would, of course, have given it to her.

Instead, the Kennedy family asked to have the book read by a number of friends and advisers. This was done, and appropriate changes were made in consultation with these distinguished friends. Mrs. Kennedy asked to have yet an-other friend read the book. This, too, was done and yet more changes were made.

However, in the last analysis, this is my book. Neither Mrs. Kennedy nor any member of the Kennedy family nor anyone else is in any way responsible for my research or the content of my work. It is my responsibility, and I am confident that my book can withstand any objective test, particularly the test of time. I ask only that it be given the chance.

When Rifkind heard about it he snapped: "I don't know about literary integrity, nor the matter of history. They don't concern me a moment. But I believe strongly in a man keeping his word, particularly when it is in a written Memorandum of Understanding." Rifkind also said that he knew of no attempt to arrange a settlement out of court, which may have made him the only person in the controversy who was unaware of one. The next afternoon the *Look* and Kennedy people met at the Century Club, a private establishment just off Fifth Avenue, and that morning galley proofs were shuttling from *Look* to Dick Goodwin in Mrs. Kennedy's apartment and back to *Look* again. Mike Land, who had edited the serialization for *Look,* was stationed in the lobby of Mrs. Kennedy's apartment building with the sole task of keeping the galleys intact. It was not much of a job, and he had whiled away the hours by talking with the Secret Service men there. Once they left on an errand after telling him to "hold the fort," and a few minutes later a ball had rolled across the lobby. The ball was followed by John Kennedy, Jr., who wanted a Secret Service man to play with him. It was, Land thought, a little sad.

When Goodwin emerged from Mrs. Kennedy's apartment, he offered Land a lift to the Century Club, and on the way there he spoke about the dispute and about himself. Wasn't it fortunate, he said, that *Look* had rejected the piece he had done on Vietnam earlier in the year? He had offered it to *The New Yorker* then, it had been accepted, and he had

made a lot more money[...]
noticed how the Manches[...]
nedy's argument with J. E[...]
(Bobby had said he knew [...]
tapping when he was Attorne[...]
only knew about it, he had co[...]

It is Goodwin's misfortune t[...]
was not hinting that Mrs. Kenn[...]
divert the nation from Bobby's p[...]
ing for something hopeful in wl[...]
However, nearly everyone in the ba[...]
trust one another by now, and near[...]
for a Machiavelli. Goodwin, who h[...]
amount of zest, did not know it but h[...]

Not that there was any place for a M[...]
as well as everyone else, was as much a vic[...]
The great white glare of publicity, the [...]
Presidential politics, and the absolute co[...]
had said what to whom were lousing up eve[...]
and feelings quite enough. A few days afte[...]
filed suit, Gardner Cowles suspected that his [...]
tapped. He had called Evan Thomas one eve[...]
own phone in his own office, and a few hours [...]
stance of the conversation found its way into a m[...]
paper. Cowles had done no more than confirm[...]
that was scheduled for the next day and to pass or[...]
of encouragement to Cass Canfield, whose resolut[...]
of the *Look* people felt, might be flagging. Still, Cc[...]
alarmed when he saw it in a newspaper and he imm[...]
called Thomas again. Had he, he asked, spoken to [...]
porter about their conversation? Thomas insisted he ha[...]
Even more alarmed now, Cowles summoned the telep[...]
company to examine his office. No bugging device was fo[...]
and in fact the newspaper story had been fortuitous, but[...]

the charg[...]
believe o[...]
The re[...]
ings bet[...]
revising[...]
happen[...]
that ap[...]
the Bc[...]
its an[...]
"a da[...]
"dra[...]
beca[...]
a pa[...]
Act[...]
the[...]
att[...]
ef[...]
d[...]
a[...]

tions, among them the London *Times, Paris-Match, Epoca* in Italy, and *Stern* in West Germany, and it had already recovered more than half the money it had paid Manchester. Consequently, the suit was now threatening not only the American but the foreign publications as well.

Above all, there was the subtle and speculative fear of Mrs. Kennedy herself, and it hung over Cowles Communications like miasma. What would the public think if America's sweetheart were forced into court to say she was being exploited by *Look* magazine? *Look* was sure that its case was sound and its moral position correct. In fact, the lawyers for Mrs. Kennedy believed they had a far stronger case against Harper & Row than against the magazine, which, after all, had not been a party to the original Memorandum of Agreement. Still, it was not enough. A court battle with Jackie could be a disaster. "Anyone who is against me will look like a rat unless I run off with Eddie Fisher," Mrs. Kennedy had said, and a vision of canceled subscriptions, letters of outrage, and quiet chuckles in the corridors of *Time-Life* spread through *Look* executives like the flu.

The first portents of a settlement came on Monday night, four days after Mrs. Kennedy had filed the suit, and they came from the Kennedy brothers. From Sun Valley, where he had just whizzed down the expert's ski trail on Rock Garden Slope, Bobby called a reporter in New York and said:

"They did not think that we could afford to sue. They did not think it to the point of not letting anybody see the manuscript they now plan to publish. This is what pushed us to the suit. We didn't want to go through a suit, and we spent a lot of time trying to avoid that."

Bobby was offering a small indication that things would be better now because the publishers had allowed the Kennedys to see the manuscript. In Boston, where he was interviewed on television, Teddy Kennedy said he was "hopeful that someday the book will be published" and that he thought there could be some kind of compromise. It was the first time a Kennedy had said such a thing since the suit was announced.

The next day, Tuesday, while Goodwin and Attwood were still debating phrases, small indications began drifting out from the Senator's people in New York that Mrs. Kennedy and *Look* were close to a settlement. By late afternoon, a few reporters were told there might be an important announcement soon. By early evening, they were told that it could come any minute, and a little later they were told to forget it, but that it would probably be the first thing the next day. In fact, it was not. Things dragged on throughout Wednesday afternoon and far into the night, and in a way it was beautiful. The battle with *Look* was ending the way it began: in confusion, publicity, and bad temper.

Early in the day Simon Rifkind said that he and David Peck would meet to "discuss a sensible package for a settlement." It was the first time Rifkind had acknowledged that a settlement was possible and it sent a host of newsmen down to Peck's office on Wall Street, where the meeting was supposed to take place. Meanwhile, the two attorneys, along with the *Look* people and Kennedy people were up in Rifkind's office on Madison Avenue, and when the word got around, the newsmen began assembling there, with the radio and television ones, of course, dragging behind all their marvelous appendages. By sunset the TV mobile units on Madison Avenue were doing a fair job of impeding traffic, the flower of the press was waiting in a corridor outside Rifkind's office, and six television cameras and nine microphones were posted near the double doors to the corridor. At 6:10 P.M. the double doors were locked. Moments later they were unlocked and a secretary came out and said:

"If there is a statement, it will be a joint statement from Mrs. Kennedy and *Look*."

By 7 P.M., Dick Goodwin was discussing the statement by telephone with Robert Kennedy in Sun Valley. Meanwhile, the ten other participants in the meeting sat around an oval wooden table and fidgeted in leather-bound chairs. Earlier that day Goodwin and Attwood had met for a last editing, and their final product was a 60,000-word serialization that had been shortened by 1,600 words. Most of the reduction was the result of rewriting and rephrasing rather than deletions, and all of it involved passages dealing with Mrs. Kennedy. There was only a single change in the first installment, and that was on a page that had not been printed. The only real problem in that first issue had been the cover, which carried a statement saying that *The Death of a President* was "the only book Mrs. John F. Kennedy asked to be written about her husband." Jackie Kennedy objected to this use of her name, but it was too late and too expensive for *Look* to print another cover. Consequently, it was agreed that the magazine could insert a statement at the end of the installment saying that neither Mrs. Kennedy nor Senator Kennedy had in any way approved the serialization.

That afternoon and early evening, Goodwin, the lawyers, and *Look* executives had settled the questions of advertising, promotion, and foreign rights. A draft agreement had been drawn up; resolution of the argument, everyone thought, was minutes away, and everyone was wrong. The Senator, still in Sun Valley, had not been consulted. He was, however, consulted endlessly as the evening wore on, mostly about the joint statement. The ashtrays overflowed on the green felt of the table. The distinguished lawyers and editors and executives shuffled their feet on the red rug and looked once again at the frieze of Christmas cards Rifkind had scattered about the office. The Senator was still being consulted about the joint statement.

"The Sun Valley command post," the men from *Look* murmured.

"Every comma, every God damn comma had to be checked," one said afterward.

Finally at 10 P.M., Gardner Cowles, the proprietor of Cowles Communications, the master of five magazines, three television and two radio stations, four newspapers and a few related enterprises, turned to Goodwin and said:

"Tell the Senator that we have been here since six and that we are not going to wait any longer."

Goodwin looked embarrassed. The joint statement was dropped. *Look* and the Senator could not agree on what it should say.

At ten thirty the double doors outside Rifkind's office swung open and there was an undignified dash in the direction of the microphones. Bill Attwood won, and in a grim voice he began reading the statement put out for Gardner Cowles:

> Following a series of meetings between Mrs. Kennedy, her advisors, and *Look* editors, several changes in the text of the *Look* serialization were mutually agreed on. These changes, involving approximately 1,600 out of 80,000 authorized words, in no way affected the historical accuracy or completeness of Mr. Manchester's manuscript.
>
> They concern only the passages to which Mrs. Kennedy objected on personal grounds.
>
> We are satisfied with the outcome of the discussions. Mr. Manchester's book is a report of great value and meaning for all Americans. I am glad this dispute is behind us and that there has been no censorship of history.
>
> As the result of our discussion with Mrs. Kennedy and her representatives, Mr. Manchester's superb job of reporting remains intact. We wish to make it clear that neither Mrs. Kennedy nor Senator Robert Kennedy nor any member of her family has in any way approved or endorsed material

appearing in *Look*'s serialization for which the publishers of *Look* assume complete and sole responsibility.

I hope that the controversy between the Kennedy family and Harper & Row will be speedily resolved because Cass Canfield has been extremely helpful in the discussions concerning the serialization.

The public should not be deprived of the opportunity to read Mr. Manchester's manuscript.

Simon Rifkind was right behind him, and he adjusted his glasses, stared down at a sheet of paper, and read:

Look magazine has agreed to remove or modify all those passages in the magazine version of *The Death of a President* relating to the personal life of Mrs. John F. Kennedy and her children. These paragraphs were the sole reasons for the initiation of her legal action.

Since every passage of a personal nature under contention for several months was either deleted by *Look,* or changed to her satisfaction Mrs. Kennedy has withdrawn her suit.

No material of historical significance has been altered, nor has the historical record been impaired in the slightest by the modifications and deletions.

Neither Mrs. Kennedy nor Senator Robert F. Kennedy has in any way approved or endorsed the material in the *Look* articles, based upon *The Death of a President.* The author, William Manchester, and the publisher of *Look* magazine have assumed complete and sole responsibility.

Mrs. Kennedy said: "I have been told there are historical inaccuracies and unfair references in this book. That they have been written is unfortunate. However, it was clear before bringing this suit that historical judgments, even if inaccurate, could not properly be suppressed by a court of law. In time, history will deal fairly and justly with this period."

Now Attwood spoke about the "historical accuracy" of Manchester's work. Jackie Kennedy, speaking through Rifkind, said she had been told of "historical inaccuracies." Clearly, these were different appraisals of history that in no way drew the two sides closer together. It did not help, either, when Dick Goodwin welcomed some reporters into Rifkind's office immediately afterward, and with the help of John Seigenthaler and Frank Mankiewicz, Bobby's press secretary, briefed them on the settlement.

Goodwin did not say anything improper, but it annoyed the *Look* executives still further. They thought, they said, there was an understanding that no one would discuss the settlement with the press. They were just as unhappy when newspapers and magazines credited Mrs. Kennedy with a smashing victory over themselves. In fact, she had not won much at all.

Ten

———————

NEARLY any millionaire can open a publishing house,
but he can hardly hope for distinction until he has
fulfilled his obligation to history and scholarship and art, and
suffered along with unknown writers. Harper & Row was
stuffed with distinction, and it knew it, and the book business knew it, and it was a sad and unhappy thing for Harper
& Row when Jacqueline Kennedy and Robert Kennedy ac-
cused it of breaking its word to them. When Cass Canfield
said that his "experience in connection with *The Death of a
President* has been the most trying and distressing one in a
forty-year publishing career," he was saying it in sorrow.

In a way, though, the fight with the Kennedys was a tri-
umph of democracy. In 1817, when J. & J. Harper published
Seneca's *Morals,* its first book, Robert Kennedy's family was
scratching about for a living in County Wexford, and years
later, when J. P. Morgan said that "it would be a national
calamity if Harper & Brothers had to go into bankruptcy,"
his grandfathers were hustling for votes in the wards and
precincts of Boston. Now, in 1966, Harper & Row was locked
in battle with the Kennedys, and for all Cass Canfield knew,
it was losing.

What made it worse, of course, was that it was so much of a family affair. Harper & Row had published John and Robert Kennedy; it had published Ted Sorensen's *Kennedy* and Paul Fay's *The Pleasure of His Company;* it was even getting ready to bring out *The Reds and the Blacks,* which would be Bill Attwood's story of his years as Ambassador in Africa, and it was, in fact, the favorite publisher of the whole Washington Establishment. Nearly forgotten among all the celebrated names Harper had handled over the years was another author it once had under contract—William Manchester.

For his master's thesis at the University of Missouri School of Journalism, Manchester had chosen the life and works of H. L. Mencken. This led him to Baltimore, a job on the Baltimore *Sun,* and a companionship with Mencken, to whom he read aloud while the old critic, sick and uncomfortable, was confined in a wheelchair. This, in turn, led Manchester to expand his master's thesis into *Disturber of the Peace: The Life of H. L. Mencken,* which he put into the hands of Don Congdon, who passed it on to Harper. Congdon had hovered between two young editors at Harper, Mike Bessie and Evan Thomas, and for no particular reason had finally given it to Bessie. Which was unfortunate; Thomas would have made history's later jape more complete.

Bessie liked the book and told Manchester so. Manchester, however, thought someone else should see it too, and so he passed it on to George Jean Nathan, Mencken's old associate on *Smart Set* and the *American Mercury.* It was a mistake. Nathan did not like the way he was portrayed in the book and immediately threatened suit against both Manchester and Harper. However, Harper stood by its author, repulsed Nathan, and saved the book. (Nathan had the last word, though. *The New York Times Sunday Book Review* asked him to review *Disturber of the Peace*. He found he did not like it.)

Manchester left Harper because he wanted to write fiction and Bessie thought his true talent lay in nonfiction. Piece by piece, Manchester kept submitting a novel called *City of Anger* to the editor, and piece by piece it was rejected. Finally, Manchester left amicably to become a foreign correspondent in India, for which *The Sun* paid him ninety-nine dollars a week, and Congdon, after a number of attempts elsewhere, found a publisher for *City of Anger* in Ballantine.

Fifteen years later, Mrs. Kennedy was a far more formidable opponent for Harper than George Jean Nathan. She could not be dismissed, and shortly after she brought the suit, Canfield solemnly put himself on record at a news conference in the Overseas Press Club. Brushing aside all questions, he had read into the microphones:

> My experience in connection with *The Death of a President* has been the most trying and distressing one in a forty-year publishing career, and Evan Thomas, the editor of the book at Harper & Row, shares my distress. We take great pride in being the publishers of President Kennedy's great book, *Profiles in Courage,* and of books by Senator Robert F. Kennedy. When the Kennedy family asked us to publish the Manchester book and we agreed to do so, they were asking us to assume the responsibilities of a publisher. It is a function we have exercised honorably and professionally over nearly one hundred and fifty years.
>
> I want to stress how very badly I feel that Mrs. Kennedy, for whom I have such deep regard and respect, is so disturbed about the book. The principals involved in this dispute are all people for whom I have deep regard and admiration and Mr. Manchester's book itself is a moving, sincere, and outstanding piece of writing. He has been subject to many repeated pressures for many months. He was asked to prepare for publication an accurate account of the events of the

assassination and he was assured that his role as an author would be respected.

Understandably, the members of the Kennedy family were unwilling to read the manuscript themselves and hence they designated representatives to do this for them. Had they read it themselves, the present situation might have been avoided.

Harper & Row was not motivated by profit when it undertook the publication of this book. On the contrary, all Harper profits will go to the Kennedy Library except for a small return to Harper's on our first printing. In no event will this limit be exceeded. Mr. Manchester is also making substantial contributions to the library from his earnings on the book. Incidentally, Harper & Row's advance to him was $40,000 and not the $675,00 erroneously reported by the press.

In the interest of historical accuracy and of the people's right to know the true facts of the awesome tragedy—the right to know which led the Kennedy family to request Mr. Manchester to write his book and us to publish it—we join with him in defending the book's right to live.

Nonsense, the Kennedys replied in a statement. "No amount of rhetoric" could alter the question of whether or not Manchester and Harper & Row had broken their word. Meanwhile, the real action then was taking place between Mrs. Kennedy and *Look,* and it was not until they announced their agreement that Harper & Row and the Kennedys settled down to the serious business of negotiations. These began with Harper & Row saying hopefully that the chances of settlement out of court were just fine. There was a feeling then that things could be resolved quickly, and of course the feeling was all wrong.

For one thing, the book was a far bulkier package than the magazine. For another, Rifkind and his assistants thought they could make a better case against Harper & Row than they could against *Look,* and so they were prepared to ask for more. Still, things might have gone quickly if Manchester had not become ill. No one really wanted the argument to end in court, but it nearly did, and it was probably no one's fault in particular; *The Death of a President* had become too big and too emotional an argument.

The day after *Look* and Mrs. Kennedy reached a settlement, the lawyers representing Harper & Row and Manchester quietly asked the court to extend the deadline under which they were supposed to file answers to Mrs. Kennedy's suit. The request was granted, and the same day Harper & Row gave Rifkind a revised manuscript of the book. Both sides solemnly agreed then that there would be no leaks to the press and no further publicity. The discussions would be kept secret.

By then, however, there was simply no chance that anything could be quiet about *The Death of a President*. Dell Books, a paperback publisher, had made an offer of one million dollars for the right to bring it out. Meanwhile, there were reports that copies of the unexpurgated manuscript had found their way to Taiwan, which has never signed an international copyright agreement, and that Chinese book pirates would publish the book and then smuggle copies into the United States. This was followed by discreet demurrals from the Chinese Nationalist Government. If *The Death of a President* was indeed on Taiwan, the government said, it would not be published. It was the first time the government had taken a position on the book pirates. Chiang Kai-shek apparently did not want to get involved.

In that week after the settlement with *Look*, Manchester was a tired and angry man. Moreover, he was ill. He was still suffering from the flu, and it got worse as the week wore on. Then, as he was trimming a Christmas tree in his home one evening, he had brushed against a pine needle and the needle had scratched the cornea of his right eye. The anger, the flu, and the flaming eye conspired to put the Kennedys, their lawyers, advisers, and spokesmen at a peculiar advantage: Manchester's approval was necessary before changes could be made in the book, they had to negotiate with him, and he did not want to negotiate.

There was by then a sort of desperation about the Kennedy people. Nothing had really worked out for them, and the controversy over the book, despite the settlement with *Look* and their devout desires, was not waning at all. *Stern,* the West German magazine that had bought the serial rights from *Look,* announced that it would publish an unexpurgated version, and *Revue,* a Dutch weekly, said that if *Stern* would it would, too.

Senator Kennedy, meanwhile, was still in Sun Valley. He, too, had decided to remain silent. A reason for this, perhaps, was that Mrs. Kennedy's suit was raising the kinds of problems that he couldn't say much about, anyway. For example, William S. White, the syndicated columnist who is a close friend of President Johnson, wrote that inescapable duty compelled him to comment on the Manchester affair and that he was doing so only with pain. Then White went on to note that since everyone knows the book would "gut Johnson," and since the Kennedys themselves had authorized it, then it was hard to see how the attacks could have been inspired by anyone other than the Kennedys. "President Johnson," White said, "has had to bear a frightful burden in the unremitting hostility of the Kennedy cult and its common attitude that the man who now sits in the White House is not simply a constitutional successor to another man slain in memorable tragedy but only a crude usurper. Every mature newspaperman in Washington knows that this is the plain truth. Every writer in the United States—and every publisher—knows, too, that the smile or the frown of the Kennedy cult has a power over the fortunes of any kind of book that this country has never known before."

Coming from a man who was supposed to know what was on the President's mind, this was strong stuff. A little later *Newsweek* said it had learned that indeed the President was disturbed by the reports about his behavior in the aftermath of the assassination. "Unhappy about the evolving portraits of himself in the stories about the Manchester book, he understands at the same time that the Kennedy set would have resented anyone who succeeded John Kennedy," said *Newsweek*.

The jest, of course, was that when *The Death of a President* appeared it was not hostile to Lyndon Johnson, and that most of the stories about the hostility had sprung from Robert Kennedy's colleagues. They had sought to show only that the Kennedys were meet and right in seeking changes in Bill Manchester's manuscript, and the stories had recoiled on them. It remained for *Time*, however, to deliver the ultimate irony. "There are already signs," it said, "that the shabby treatment of Lyndon Johnson might create a backlash of public sympathy for him."

Clearly, something had to be done. Goodwin, Rifkind, and Seigenthaler, who were representing Mrs. Kennedy in New York, were being overtaken by politics. Mrs. Kennedy, who had first announced that she would spend the days after Christmas in Sun Valley with Robert Kennedy and his family, had changed her mind and was preparing to fly to Antigua with her children. Manchester was still adamant; he was tired of the whole thing, sick besides, and impervious to entreaties from his publisher. The only possibility was that an intermediary could move between the Kennedys and the author, and the only possibility for that job was Don Congdon.

Nonetheless, Goodwin, Rifkind, and Seigenthaler turned

to him only reluctantly. Although he had played no role in the negotiations with either *Look* or Harper & Row, Goodwin and Seigenthaler, at least, thought of him as something of a gray eminence behind Manchester. In fact he was not; he was only his long-time friend and agent. Congdon first became involved in settling the dispute on the Friday before Christmas at a meeting in the Harper & Row board room. Henceforth, he would bargain off a phrase in the text here for a point of fact there, an inflection on one page for a subtlety on another. It was a trading situation.

The next day the negotiators met for lunch at the Century Club. They were hopeful. Seigenthaler and Goodwin had begun to think that Congdon was a man they could work with, and there was even a sort of joviality. Seigenthaler baited Evan Thomas ("Evan, did you *really* think that telegram from Bob meant approval?"), Thomas told Seigenthaler a little stiffly that he would be surprised by the affidavit that had been prepared for him by Harper's attorneys, and Goodwin and Congdon smelled at each other's cigars. Meanwhile, in Middletown, Connecticut, Manchester, who had not been feeling well all week, began to feel even worse. The next day, Christmas, his temperature began to climb, and late that night he was admitted to Middlesex Memorial Hospital in Middletown. He had a temperature of 104.2, with a pneumonia infection in the lower left lung, and he was placed on the critical list.

A man who works for the Senator, and who absolutely refuses to be identified, says the report that Manchester was on the critical list cleaved his heart with an icy finger of dread. "Christ," he says, "I thought we'd killed him." The day after Manchester was admitted, however, the hospital took him off the critical list and his temperature dropped nearly to normal. A flock of reporters showed up to skulk about the hospital grounds, and from Sun Valley and Antigua Bobby and Jackie Kennedy sent telegrams urging him to get well. Mrs. Kennedy, meanwhile, was finding only a fitful peace on the island. The same day she sent the telegram to Manchester, two photographers had come upon her and her children while they were swimming, and she had yelled for her Secret Service agents, who waded in and chased them. Later, after they had mistakenly seized the wrong two photographers, the police posted guards near the ocean-front estate where Mrs. Kennedy was staying, and one of her companions had announced:

"Mrs. Kennedy is irked. She had demanded complete privacy."

Manchester's illness handicapped the moves toward a settlement, of course, but it could not halt them. The lawyers were making their own way. On December 27, the day Justice Streit had chosen for the hearing when Mrs. Kennedy first filed suit, the attorneys for both Manchester and Harper & Row asked him to postpone it. He agreed, and Carleton Eldridge, Manchester's lawyer, suggested that the case against his client be heard January 16. Streit agreed again, and then Edward S. Greenbaum, the counsel for Harper & Row, asked blandly that the case against the publisher be heard the very next day, December 28. Greenbaum said later that he had asked for the early hearing only because "we want to have the temporary injunction (against publication) disposed of promptly, that's all." Rifkind, however, had understood beforehand that both Greenbaum and Eldridge would ask for a hearing in the middle of January, and he said with some annoyance that Greenbaum's request was simply beyond his comprehension. Most courtroom observers, however, concluded that Greenbaum was just trying to speed up the negotiations and that he believed Rifkind and Mrs. Kennedy would be happy to speed them up to avoid a battle in open court.

Nonetheless, that afternoon, after he had conferred with Rifkind, Greenbaum, too, asked for a hearing in the middle of January, and he and Rifkind put out a statement. It said that representatives of Harper and Mrs. Kennedy "have been making steady progress toward a settlement" and therefore it was agreed that the trial date should be postponed. "The sole object of this arrangement," it said, "is to give all parties, including the author, sufficient time for thorough discussion."

In a way, the failure of the case to ever go through open court was a loss to legal scholarship; it could have established an interesting precedent. Mary Hemingway had tried to prevent the publication of A. E. Hotchner's *Papa Hemingway* by saying that the author had appropriated material she considered part of her husband's legacy. She lost the case. Mrs. Kennedy was trying to prevent the publication of *The Death of a President* by charging that the author had breached a contract. The issue seemed to be simple, and it was not.

If the court found that she had approved the manuscript, then, of course, the book could be published. However, even if it found that she had not, it could not be guaranteed that an injunction could be issued and then allowed to stand by a higher court. Irwin Karp, the legal representative for the Author's League of America, wondered during the dispute if the Constitution did not prohibit a court from enforcing a contract such as Manchester had signed. He thought there was at least a possibility that the right of free speech might take precedent over the right of a contract, and in an article in *The Saturday Review* he argued that everyone would be better off if it did. Other attorneys noted that damages, not injunctions, were the usual remedy in suits for breach of contract.

Aside from any constitutional issue, the case had a lovely flavor of ambiguity all its own. The Senator had sent a telegram saying that "members of the Kennedy family would

place no obstacle in the way of publication of the book."
But in the affidavit he filed with Mrs. Kennedy's suit he said
that he had not waived his right to approve the manuscript in
the telegram, and that even if he had he certainly could not
have waived Mrs. Kennedy's right. Still, the legal effect of
the telegram depended on half-remembered conversations
and actions before and after it was sent, and so did the question of whether or not the Senator was speaking for Mrs.
Kennedy.

In general, one person cannot speak for another person
without express approval, but if Mrs. Kennedy, by her actions, seemed to give the Senator the approval, then she
could be held to the consequences of his actions. For instance,
Pamela Turnure had told Manchester that the Senator would
handle things for Mrs. Kennedy. Furthermore, Mrs. Kennedy
herself had never asked to see the manuscript. Harper & Row
and Manchester could note these things, and say that Mrs.
Kennedy had therefore waived her own right of approval.
Then, presumably, they would argue that, besides sending
the telegram, Senator Kennedy had told a number of persons
that the book ought to be published in 1966, not 1968, as the
Memorandum of Understanding had stipulated. (Among the
persons he told it to was Marquis Childs, the columnist.
Childs, in fact, was prepared to file an affidavit and say so.)
Furthermore, Evan Thomas claimed that at the stormy meeting in August among Manchester, Seigenthaler, Kennedy,
and himself, the Senator had drawn him aside and told him
not to worry, to go ahead and get the book out.

Then there was the problem of all the readers, of the
committee system that was used to edit *The Death of a
President*. Some authorities thought it could be argued that
the inartistically drawn Memorandum of Understanding did
not provide that a platoon would be enlisted by the Kennedys
to approve the manuscript. The Kennedys, they said, had to

do it themselves. The suit was really a can of worms, and like the argument itself it was never very simple.

Manchester himself didn't know how complicated it was until the afternoon of December 31 when he left the hospital. His wife drove him home, and when he arrived there he conferred by phone with his attorneys. He had always considered the evidence on his side to be beyond interpretation or dispute, and he had reckoned that Harper & Row saw it precisely as he did. Then he found it was not quite so, and it was, he recalled later, "a bleak, bleak day."

He was absolutely sure, for instance, that on July 14 John Seigenthaler had called Evan Thomas and told him that the manuscript was now approved. Thomas, however, did not seem prepared to say this in court. Manchester was also certain that Kennedy's telegram in July confirmed that the manuscript had been fully approved. In his affidavit, Cass Canfield was saying that he considered the telegram to be a sign that the book could be released sometime in 1967. It did not mention approval. Furthermore, Manchester discovered that some of the correspondence Thomas sent to the Kennedys was somewhat ambiguous, that it could be interpreted to mean that Harper & Row did not consider the manuscript fully approved, even after the Senator's telegram.

Manchester's attorneys were unhappy, too, and they talked of the great fidelity Harper & Row was showing to the Kennedys, even in the teeth of a lawsuit. Meanwhile, revisions in the manuscript were still being made, mostly by Congdon, Goodwin, and Thomas. Congdon says that no violence was done to the book, and that what was taken out was trivia, but he also admits that the Kennedys were getting all the best of it, and that he was able to win few points for Manchester.

All that was happening in New York was happening away from public view, but nearly anything about *The Death of a President* was captivating, and when *Stern,* the West German weekly, announced that it would publish the unexpurgated version of the serialization there sprang up another great peripheral issue. *Look*, by then, had sold the serialization rights in twenty-five countries. The magazines that bought them after the settlement with Mrs. Kennedy had received the edited version, but *Stern*, which had paid $72,500 for the rights, had been one of the first to buy and it had received the same material that *Look* had intended to use. Henri Nannen, the editor of *Stern*, insisted that the revisions in the serialization were made for political and not personal reasons, and that it was his duty, therefore, to publish them.

Consequently, *Stern* received a telegram from Robert Kennedy saying that publication of the deletions would "cause distress" to Mrs. Kennedy. The chairman of the Committee for Science, Culture and Publications in the German Bundestag told Nannen that he could see no convincing reason to disregard Mrs. Kennedy's wishes, and *Look* said that it would take "appropriate action" to prevent *Stern* from using the expurgated material. It was all to no avail, and on January 9, the same day that *Look* appeared with its first installment of *The Death of a President*, so did *Stern*.

Look had known there would be an enormous demand for its installments. It had not, however, known just how enormous it would be. Within a few hours after they went on sale, 4,000 copies were sold in the Times Square area alone. United Airlines received 1,800 copies for use in its planes and terminals and within twenty-four hours they had all been lifted from their binders and taken by passengers. In Mexico City, the black market price for the first issue went to fifty pesos, and a dealer in the Wall Street area found that he could get one dollar for it. The advertising manager for Prudential Insurance lost his briefcase on the Lackawanna Railroad and within the briefcase was a copy of *Look*. When he retrieved it from the lost-and-found office in Hoboken only the magazine was missing. The administrative assistant for a West Virginia Congressman called the *Look* circulation department to say that one of the Congressman's constituents, a news-dealer, had not received his twelve copies, and where were they? There were innumerable giggling calls from "Bobby Kennedy's office" saying that the Senator hadn't gotten his copy, and one from a lady who said her poodle had chewed up just *The Death of a President*, leaving the other pages intact. A whimsical girl in the circulation department sent her tear sheets.

The installments also reached the losers, the eccentrics, and all the sad people who had convinced themselves that they were part of the legend of John Kennedy. A man sent in a transcript of a talk he once had with the spirit world: "Hello, come in JFK," "Yes, this is JFK." Women called to say they had once been married to John Kennedy, and a perfectly doctored photograph of him sitting in a tree watching his own funeral in Arlington arrived in the mail.

Immediately after the first issue of *Stern* appeared, socially prominent William vanden Heuvel, who had been an of-ficial in the Justice Department under Robert Kennedy, volunteered to go to Hamburg for the Kennedys to reason with the German publishers. He invoked the feelings of Mrs. Kennedy with the Germans, and he was not notably success-ful. *Look* sent Bill Attwood, who noted that *Stern* had broken an earlier agreement with *Look* not to publish anything before January 15, five days after the first *Look* installment was to appear, and had published on January 9. Eventually, after it had brought out the entire first installment in two successive issues, *Stern* capitulated.

In New York, meanwhile, the argument over *The Death of a President* was inching toward a conclusion. Nettlesome problems persisted. As part of a settlement, the Kennedys wanted it understood that Manchester would never again write about the assassination. Furthermore, they wanted it understood in writing. Carleton Eldridge and Paul Gitlin, the attorney for Manchester's literary agents, told Rifkind and Goodwin that certainly they would put it in the agreement. It would say: "William Manchester will never again write about the assassination, *nor could he.*"

The implication, of course, was that Manchester had been so driven and burdened that he couldn't have done it anyway.

Goodwin looked up, waggled a finger at Rifkind, and they withdrew from the room. When they returned, Rifkind said, "I have a dramatic announcement to make," and then yielded on the demand.

Perhaps the most difficult problem, though, involved money. If *The Death of a President* were to be published, money would surround it in wads and bales. There was going to be an embarrassment of money, and everyone knew it. Even before the first rumblings had been heard from Hyannisport, Harper & Row had felt that Manchester's book could be an extraordinary financial success, and the $250,000 offer from the Book-of-the-Month Club for the right to distribute it, and the one-million-dollar offer from Dell for the right to put it in paperback had confirmed the feeling.

Nonetheless, from the very beginning Harper & Row had insisted that it did not want to commercialize the assassination, and Harper & Row was serious. The original agreement with the Kennedys had allowed the publisher to keep a normal profit on the first 45,000 copies, plus a quarter of the book club money and a quarter of the paperback money. But now, locked in a suit with the Kennedys and wanting only to get out, Harper amplified an earlier offer it had made to the Kennedys: it would renounce the money from the Book-of-the-Month Club and from a paperback publisher, and it would keep only a modest profit of 6 percent after taxes of its net receipts on the first 100,000 copies. This would be about $38,000.

Harper & Row said it would take no further profit beyond this. It would, however, receive "overhead expenses" on all copies it sold, including the first 100,000. Since Manchester had already limited himself to a royalty on only the first 100,000 hardcover copies, the Kennedy Memorial Library would get the entire profit on all the other books. With a first printing of 600,000 copies, it would be a considerable amount of money. Moreover, with Harper & Row happy to surrender its share of the money from a possible paperback publication and the Book-of-the-Month Club, the library would gain an enormous windfall.

The Kennedys, however, were skeptical about a sale to a paperback publisher. What might happen to *The Death of a President* then? A screaming cover? A foreword saying God knows what? Lurid pictures? Morbid diagrams? The possibilities were endless. Moreover, the Kennedys did not want the book involved in anything else that touched on a huge sum of money. The one-million-dollar offer by Dell indicated that the commercialization of the assassination was getting out of hand. Robert Kennedy ruled that, if a paperback edition had to be published, then Harper & Row would publish it under its own imprint, and then either distribute it itself or through another paperback reprint publisher.

Harper & Row was agreeable. It had already parted with what would have been an immense profit from the hardcover sales and the book club royalties. Now it would forgo the sale to a paperback publisher and put out the paperback itself, paying a royalty of 5 percent to the library and 5 percent to Manchester. Harper & Row would take no profit from this, but would again recover its overhead expenses, as it would on the hardcover version. But how does a publisher determine in December what his expenses will be a year hence? One way is to turn to the statistics put out annually by the American Book Publishers' Council, which draws them from reports that are supplied voluntarily by many of its members. In the council's report for 1965, the average overhead cost to a paperbound publisher was 41.1 percent of the price at which a book was sold by the publisher to his dealers. Similarly, the council's report for 1965 indicated the average overhead expense for a hardcover publisher to be 44.9 percent of the price at which a book was sold to dealers. In determining the overhead expenses on *The Death of a President,* Harper & Row and the Kennedys accepted the figures from the Book Publishers' Council as fair, and in a further burst of generosity Harper & Row agreed to consider its expenses as even less than the council's figures suggested. Harper & Row said it would compute its overhead on both the hardcover and the paperback at a flat 40 percent.

This was fine, and it appeared that the Kennedys and the publisher had found a way to prevent the further commercialization of *The Death of a President.* Still, consider the figures reported by the Book Publishers' Council, particularly the ones on paperback costs; they are misleading. Overhead expenses are closely guarded secrets in the mass-market paperback industry, and none of the highly competitive, mass-market paperback publishers had contributed to the 1965 survey of the Book Publishers' Council. The only figures available, therefore, were those for the quality, high-priced paperback lines, such as Harper's own Torchbooks. These quality paperback sales are small by mass-market standards. They are measured in the thousands, not the hundreds of thousands, and they are made largely through college and trade bookstores. Quality paperback publishers cannot use the mass distribution techniques of the mass-market paperback publishers and they have far higher overhead and distribution expenses than do the mass-market houses. Most mass-market houses have overhead and distribution costs far below the 41.1 percent figure put out by the American Book Publishers' Council.

Then there is Harper's 40 percent overhead on the hardcover edition. The book will probably be sold to retailers and wholesalers at about 45 percent off the $10 list price, for a gross of $5.50 a copy. Forty percent of this is $2.20, and a sale of 600,000 copies means that Harper's would receive $1,320,000 for overhead expenses. However, the figures on overhead from the Book Publishers' Council are an industry average, and all publishers agree that they cannot be applied to a single book that would sell 600,000 copies at $10 a copy. On such a book, an industry average would be meaningless. What is an accurate estimate of Harper's costs? Several publishers have suggested that an actual cost would be about $300,000. However, Harper & Row had extraordinary additional expenses connected with *The Death of a President:* legal fees, plane trips, a quick visit to London by Cass Canfield and Evan Thomas. Allowing a realistic $100,000 for these, it is still fair to estimate Harper & Row's "nonprofit" as about $920,000 before taxes on the hardcover edition of the book.

The extraordinary thing about all this was that Harper's goodness and the Kennedys' determination to see that *The Death of a President* was not commercialized almost certainly did what they were not supposed to do: They diverted large sums of money away from the library and toward Harper & Row and William Manchester. For example, Dell had offered one million dollars as an advance against royalties, a sum that could be surpassed by royalties on the paperback edition. If the offer had been accepted, the Kennedy Library would have been guaranteed $750,000—the share it was entitled to under the original contract with Harper, plus the quarter share that Harper had agreed to surrender. Moreover, in the heady atmosphere that surrounded *The Death of a President,* the royalties could easily surpass a one-million-dollar advance. In publishing, a rule of thumb is that the paperback sale of a book should be at least ten times its hardcover sale. If the book sold 600,000 copies in hardcover, it would not be unreasonable to hope for a sale of six million in paperback. Since the hardcover book contained nearly 400,000 words of text spread over 710 large pages, a paperback edition would run about a thousand pages. Manufacturing costs alone on this bulky a paperback would be about twenty-three cents apiece, even in quantities of a million copies. While it might be possible to sell the paperback at $1.45, it was more likely to sell for $1.65. Dell said later that it regarded a 15 percent royalty as almost certain on the paperback edition, and that it might have agreed to an even higher rate.

Therefore, if *The Death of a President* sold six million copies in paperback at, say, $1.45 a copy, the Kennedy Library's share of a 15 percent royalty—its half, plus the quarter that Harper & Row was surrendering—would have been $978,750. Under the new agreement the Kennedys negotiated with Harper & Row, however, the library's 5 percent royalty on a similar sale would amount to $435,000, a "loss" to the library of $543,750. If the paperback sold six million copies at $1.65, the library would have received $1,113,750 under the old arrangement. Under the new one it would get $495,000, a loss of $618,750.

An obvious irony of this agreement was that some of the money drifting away from the Kennedy Library was going toward Bill Manchester, for whom, presumably, the Kennedys, their advisers, and spokesmen had small use. Under the original agreement, he would have got a quarter of the paperback royalties. Under the new one he would be paid a straight 5 percent royalty. Therefore, if his book were to sell six million paperback copies at $1.45, he would have got $326,250 under the old arrangement; under the new one he would get $435,000, a gain of $108,750. If the paperback sold six million copies at $1.65, he would have got $371,250 under the old arrangement; under the new one he would get $495,000 for a gain of $123,750.

It is illogical that the Kennedys would accept an arrangement that would give the author more and the library less, but then everything about the Manchester affair was illogical. The great illogicalness, however, was left for Harper & Row. It had said with deep feeling that it did not want to make money on the assassination, and it had sought earnestly to surrender its potential profit on a paperback edition. After the argument with Mrs. Kennedy was ended it even announced that its total profit from *The Death of a President* would be $38,000. Nevertheless, consider the figures arising from the new contract that the Kennedys' advisers and Harper & Row negotiated in December. In time they could burden the publisher with money. Harper & Row was to figure its overhead expenses for the paperback at 40 percent. That means 40 percent of the price it received from selling the paperback to distributors. A standard figure in publishing is that paperbacks are sold to distributors at discounts that average about 45 percent from the price marked on the book. Therefore, if Harper & Row sold six million copies of *The Death of a President* in paperback at $1.45 a copy, their receipts from the sale would be about $4,785,000. Of this, 40 percent, or $1,914,000, would be kept by Harper & Row for overhead expenses.

But what would Harper's actual expenses be? The major expense in publishing a single paperback in such quantity would be that of distributing and shipping. Mass-market publishers figure their own average cost of distribution is about 6 percent of the cover price. Harper & Row, of course, might have to pay another publisher more to distribute a Harper book, but there is great competition among mass-market paperback publishers to distribute best sellers such as *The Death of a President*. The best sellers help publishers to better display their entire line, and it is an educated guess that Harper & Row will not pay more than 10 percent of the cover price to another publisher to distribute a Harper paperback edition of *The Death of a President*. If six million copies were sold at $1.45 a copy, Harper's cost of distribution could be as high as $870,000. Harper could then be left with a profit before taxes of as much as $1,044,000.

If the edition sold for more, say, $1.65, it would make comparably more. If six million copies were sold at $1.65, Harper's net profit could be $1,188,000 before taxes. Of course, Harper & Row had said the library would get all the profits from a paperback, and it would. But consider the profit.

The gross receipts to a publisher from a sale of six million copies would be $4,785,000. From this must be subtracted the overhead of $1,914,000, as well as $870,000 in royalties, manufacturing costs of approximately $1,518,000, and shipping costs of $198,000. (The manufacturing expenses can be computed by figuring the cost of manufacturing 6,600,000 copies at twenty-three cents apiece, the 600,000 extra copies being a minimal estimate for damaged and unsold copies. The shipping costs would be about three cents apiece for all 6,600,000 copies.) The profit left to the Kennedy Library is then no more than a modest $285,000. Add to this the 5 percent royalty, $435,000, and the total is some $278,000 short of the $978,000 the library would have received under the old agreement.

If the paperback edition were published at $1.65, the results would be better: a gross of $5,445,000, less an overhead of $2,178,000, royalties of $990,000, and the same manufacturing and shipping charges as on the $1.45 edition. The net profit would be $561,000. Add to this the royalty on the $1.65 edition, $495,000, and the total for the library is $1,056,000, still some $57,750 below what it would have received if Dell had published the paperback.

On January 16, 1967, Justice Streit issued a judgment and decree that ended the case of Jacqueline Kennedy against Harper & Row and William Manchester. The settlement, which cost *The Death of a President* about seven pages of text, had been expected for days, but it was not until the small hours of that morning, when Mrs. Kennedy put the manuscript aside after reading it for the first time herself, that anyone could be sure the argument was really over. Justice Streit decreed that Manchester would surrender the tape-recorded interviews he had made with Jacqueline and Robert Kennedy and that he would be allowed to keep no more than two manuscript copies of his book. Harper & Row would be allowed to publish the now approved manuscript and to have it distributed through the Book-of-the-Month Club and then brought out in paperback. In a statement, the participants in the suit said:

> Mrs. John F. Kennedy, Harper & Row, and William Manchester have resolved the differences which led to legal action. Certain personal passages of concern to Mrs. Kennedy have been deleted or modified by mutual agreement of all the parties. Therefore, Mrs. Kennedy has terminated her lawsuit. All parties agree that the historical record has not been censored in any way.
>
> While the settlement regarding the book is satisfactory to all concerned, the parties regret that the questions in dispute could not have been earlier settled. A number of problems arising over a period of several months had to be resolved.
>
> Harper & Row will in April publish William Manchester's book, *The Death of a President,* in accordance with arrangements made at the outset.

In the weeks that followed, it was estimated that Manchester, even though he was turning over a major share of his earnings to the Kennedy Library, might make as much as $500,000 after taxes from his book. In time, it was thought, the library would get more than five million dollars. "The library ought to put up a statue to Bill Manchester," said Paul Gitlin, one of the lawyers who had argued for the author. Robert Kennedy, however, did not see it that way. "They've got the money," he told Dick Goodwin, "and we've got the public relations problem." It was not really surprising then, when Mrs. Kennedy canceled the Government allowance she had been receiving for her Park Avenue office, or when she granted her first newspaper interview since the assassination. It was carried in three parts by a New York newspaper, which called it "a story that is part of our times," and it was all mush. Contemplating things one evening not long afterward, William Manchester wondered aloud: "What would happen if someone started a rumor that I was writing a novel about the Kennedys?" It was almost too much to consider.